FIRE AND FUELS
R.A. CARE

Drawings by Alec Davis

London

First published in Great Britain 1975 by
Mills & Boon Limited, 17–19 Foley Street, London W1A 1DR

R. A. Care 1975

ISBN 0 263 05593 0

All rights reserved. No part of this publication may be reproduced, stored in a retrieval system, or transmitted in any form or by any means, electronic, mechanical, photocopying, recording or otherwise, without the prior permission of Mills & Boon Limited

Book designed by Alec Davis
Made and printed in Great Britain by
Thomson Litho, East Kilbride, Scotland

CONTENTS

Chapter		Page
	Introduction	5
1	Early uses of fire	9
2	Ancient stories and superstitions	21
3	What is *burning*?	28
4	Early ideas about the nature of fire	37
5	Flames	48
6	What has energy to do with burning?	66
7	When speed is vital	71
8	Coal	92
9	Oil	106
10	Gas	122
11	Electricity	137
12	Fire, the bad master	149
13	The great fire of London	158
14	Fire in war	165

'I'm taking back my gift of fire.'

INTRODUCTION

WHERE WOULD WE BE WITHOUT FIRE?

We use fire and the energy it provides so readily and reliably in our lives that we tend to take it for granted. Just how important is it? Does it merely help to keep us warm and get rid of the rubbish? Is it a bit more important than that? Could we live for long without it?

One way to answer these questions is to try to picture what would happen if the gift of fire was taken back. 'Impossible!' you say—and you are probably right. However, suppose you got up one morning and, as you went into the kitchen looking for breakfast, you met a strong, rather ugly man wearing a white shirt and cap, leaning on a wooden crutch.

'I'm taking back my gift of fire,' he says.
'Why? And who are you anyway?' might be your reply.
'That's the whole point,' says the stranger. 'I am the god of fire. I've been known as Hephaistos and as Vulcan but, now everyone uses fire, no one knows me and no one thanks me. I'm fed up with all of you and I'm taking it back!' So saying, he limps out through the wall to give your neighbours the same message.

The gas fire goes out and so does the cooker (turn the gas off, quick!). If you have an oil heater or a coal fire, they go out, too. An electric power cut follows as the generators in the coal- and oil-fuelled power stations stop turning. The demand is too great for the power stations running on nuclear energy to cope with, so they cut out, too.

You can only have a cold breakfast. Your home is getting chilly but you can put on more clothes to keep warm.

Time to go to school; it is safe to ride a bicycle today. No cars can run, even though their batteries are charged and their tanks are full, because the petrol will not burn in their engines. No trains can move either; electric, diesel-electric, diesel-hydraulic, they all rely on fire somewhere. School won't be very full today. Tempers grow short because morning cigarettes and pipes will not light.

So far, the loss of fire has been a nuisance to you, but it is much worse for others. Aeroplanes plunge from the sky, out of control as their jet engines die; steam ships drift helplessly wherever the sea chooses. Only sailing ships and a few nuclear-powered vessels can keep on course. Infantry charging into battle would be surprised that enemy machine guns had stopped firing. They would not have time to think about the grenades rolling at their feet without exploding, before they were fighting desperately with bayonets, their own firearms proving equally useless.

News of the effects in other parts of the country of the loss of fire only comes slowly. Because no electricity comes from the power stations, no transmitters are working, so even portable radios are useless; the phone will not work, and newspapers are no longer being printed.

Supplies of processed foods, cleaning materials, fabrics and clothes would all run out. Industry would be at a standstill. Serious epidemics would break out in the cities with their inhabitants weakened by cold and hunger, and unable to collect and dump all their rubbish.

Adapting to the situation, the few nuclear power stations could be started up again to provide electricity for the areas round them. Some generators could be powered by waterwheels in fast-moving rivers, and the wind could be harnessed on bleak moors and mountains. While people in these fortunate areas would probably be able to regain a comfortable, productive life, others would be forced to move to a warmer climate and try to live off the land.

This book will help you to find out what fire really is, and how its vital force was tamed and harnessed to serve our daily needs, so that it has eventually become an almost irreplaceable part of our lives.

THINGS TO DO

Make a list of all the things you eat, wear or use during the day, which need fire at some stage or other to prepare them. These are the things you would have to do without or which could not be replaced when they wear out, if all fire was taken away. Try to work out how you could keep yourself alive, fed and comfortable in a world without fire. If several of you are doing this (e.g. at school) you might like to turn it into a play.

Introduction

ABOUT THE EXPERIMENTS IN THIS BOOK

Please do not play with fire. In Chapters 3 and 5 I have described experiments you can do with lighted candles. As I repeat there, you must make sure a responsible adult knows exactly what you are doing before you try them. Please do not use them as a lead into general fun and games with fire. You may do a lot of damage and get hurt yourself. Remember, FIRE IS DANGEROUS.

The earliest users of fire, as they may have appeared in the mouth of a cave of Choukoutien about half a million years ago. The food of these Peking Men included venison and berries. (British Museum, Natural History)

1 EARLY USES OF FIRE

HOW IT ALL BEGAN

Half a million years ago there were some nearly-human beings living in a limestone cave at Choukoutien near Peking. They differed from their close relatives, the apes, in that they walked upright, they chipped stones to make crude tools and they tended a fire in their cave home. They were the earliest people we know to have used fire.

Not many clues have survived about what people did that long ago, so we cannot hope to find out for sure how primitive people tamed fire and learned to use it. However, you can imagine yourself in their position and try to picture what probably happened.

Because you had no fire to keep you warm in cold weather, you had to live in a tropical region, though you may have worn animal skins or a strip of bark for some protection. You lived with all your relatives as a large family or tribe. You ate fruit, nuts and young shoots. Any meat came from animals which you hunted with spears or a club—and you ate it raw. Any fires which you saw were ones which had started naturally, perhaps by lightning striking a tree, or by volcanic lava, or by sparks from a rolling stone bouncing down a mountainside.

Other animals would be afraid of fire and would avoid it: presumably you would too, at first. But you would also be a hungry animal and a curious one. The aroma from the roasted carcass of an animal overtaken by a fire would lead you to find cooked meat more tender and tasty than raw meat. Perhaps you would drag home a smouldering branch which the tribe could investigate. Because none of you would know how to make fire, it would be necessary to find out how to keep this one alight but under control—let's hope you would be successful   with dry sticks to make it blaze up and greenery to damp it down, yet not letting it choke in its own ashes.

Once you had learned how to keep your fire burning steadily, you were no longer dependent on chance outbreaks. By carrying a piece of

Early uses of fire

smouldering wood or bark with you, you could start a fresh fire wherever you needed it. So you were able to keep warm, cook your food and drive away troublesome insects and wild animals.

With fire to keep him warm, man, the tropical animal, was able to spread to cooler parts of the world, urged on by the need for more hunting ground as tribes increased in size and number.

Even today, primitive tribesmen hardly ever put out their camp fires when they move on. Probably the earliest men did not put out their fires either. More likely, they banked the fire up in case they returned: thus they could always go back for a fresh light if the one they carried with them went out. Inevitably, fires left like this would sometimes set fire to the surrounding country.

Apart from accidental fires of this sort, ancient man probably set fire to jungles and woods deliberately in order to open up land. You would find it difficult to hunt in thick forests or dense jungles because the animals would have too much cover and you would only be able to move along narrow trails. You would find it dangerous, too, because you might well find yourself hunted by hungry animals or by human enemies.

Burning away the dense underbush of the forest left much less cover for the animals and they could be hunted more easily. Burning areas of brush made better grassland possible, which, in turn, produced more game. By making regular fire drives for clearing trees and bushes, killing insects, and driving animals towards waiting hunters, men changed the appearance of large areas of the earth's surface, changing them from dense forest to open grassland. The North American prairies, the South American pampas, the Russian steppes and the African veld were probably all cleared in this way.

(opposite)
Erupting volcanoes provided an opportunity for early men to learn the secrets of fire. (Keystone Press Agency)

You can see that trees grow well here, where they are allowed to do so, lining the roads.
This Manitoba prairie land was probably cleared of its original covering of forest by burning in prehistoric times. Repeated burning would have been necessary to prevent the trees growing again, until recent times when the land became farmed systematically. (National Film Board of Canada photograph)

Early uses of fire

HOW MEN FIRST LIT THEIR OWN FIRES

By seizing these advantages which fire gave, your tribe would, in time, come to depend on their fire. Until someone discovered a way of starting fresh fires whenever he wanted, you can see what a disaster it would be if your tribe's fire went out. The step from controlling a fire collected from a natural outbreak to making one's own fire was great and must have taken hundreds of thousands of years.

A fire plough being used to light a fire in New Guinea. (Radio Times Hulton Picture Library)

Lighting a fire by rubbing wood

The most widespread and probably the oldest methods depend on the heat produced when two pieces of wood are rubbed together. Possibly someone got the idea when he saw a fire started by tree branches rubbing together as they swayed in the wind.

The Australian aborigines, New Zealand Maoris and many other primitive people made fire by ploughing one piece of wood repeatedly along the grain of another, making a groove. Another way is to saw with a stick across the grain of another piece of wood which serves as the hearth. Yet another way is to use a drill-stick. In its simplest form a man presses a drill-stick into a shallow pit in a horizontal piece of wood which serves as a hearth. He twists the stick rapidly backwards and forwards between his hands until the wood dust produced in the hearth smoulders. Then he blows on it till it bursts into flame.

Experiment 1: How to do it yourself. Try this primitive method of making fire which is used by the Eskimos—but make sure a grown-up knows what you are doing, in case you are too successful! Remember that even a small fire can easily grow into a dangerous one.

Cut a straight stick about 2 cm ($\frac{3}{4}$ inch) in diameter and about 30 cm (1 ft) long. Sharpen both ends. This serves as a drill.

Cut a shallow hole in a flat piece of dry wood, in which one end of your drill-stick can spin. This will be your hearth.

Make a bow from another long stick and some stout cord.

The only other article needed is a bearing for the top of the drill so that you can steady it and press it into the hearth while it is spinning. A pebble with a hole in will do nicely.

Wind the bow-string once or twice round the drill-stick. Steady the hearth with one foot. Press the stick down into the hole in the hearth and spin it by drawing the bow backwards and forwards: see Figure 1.

After about a minute, you will probably find a steady stream of smoke coming from the bottom of the drill, and a pile of blackened, powdered wood collecting round the edge of the hole. If you can make this dust smoulder on its own you have mastered the art of making fire. Try different types of wood to see which produces the best result.

Early uses of fire

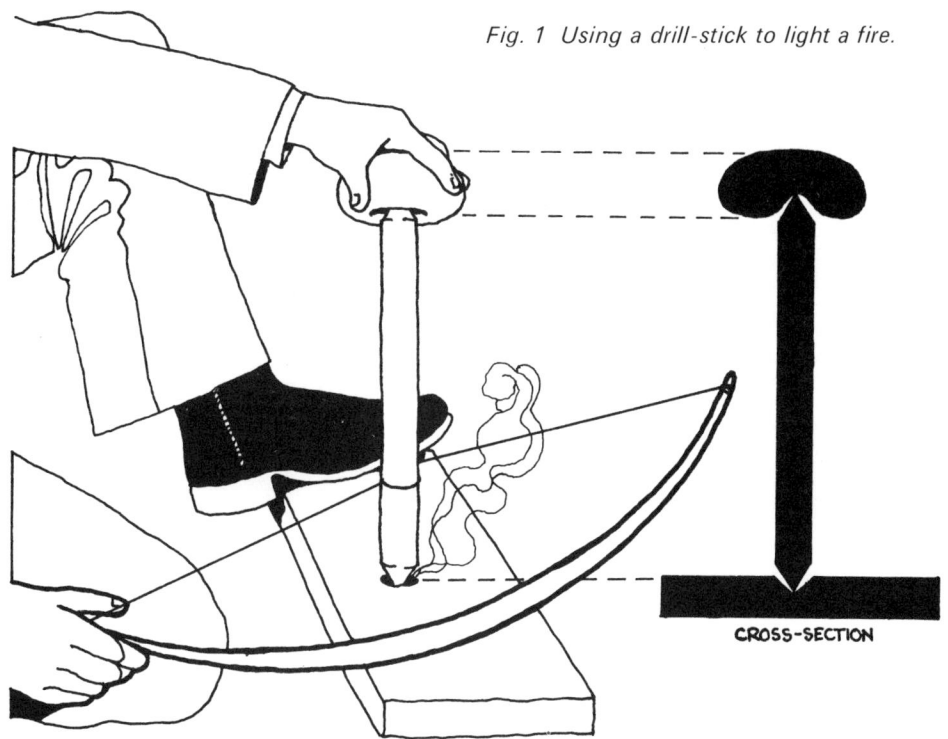

Fig. 1 Using a drill-stick to light a fire.

Fire pistons
Air always gets hotter when it is compressed suddenly—that is why the bottom end of your pump grows warm when you pump up your bicycle tyres.

Experiment 2: You will feel the rise in temperature of a bicycle pump more if you close the hole at the end of the pump tightly with one finger and then try to pump air past your finger, so that it makes a loud squeal. Inhabitants of Indonesia and the Philippines invented and used fire pistons which produced heat and fire by compressing air in a small bamboo tube with a tight-fitting piston, rather like your bicycle pump with the end blocked. Some material which would catch fire easily, tinder, was attached either to the bottom of the piston or to the cylinder. It ignited when the piston was pressed downwards and removed smartly.

Using the sun
Other ancient methods of lighting fires depend on concentrating the sun's rays onto one spot, thereby making it very hot.

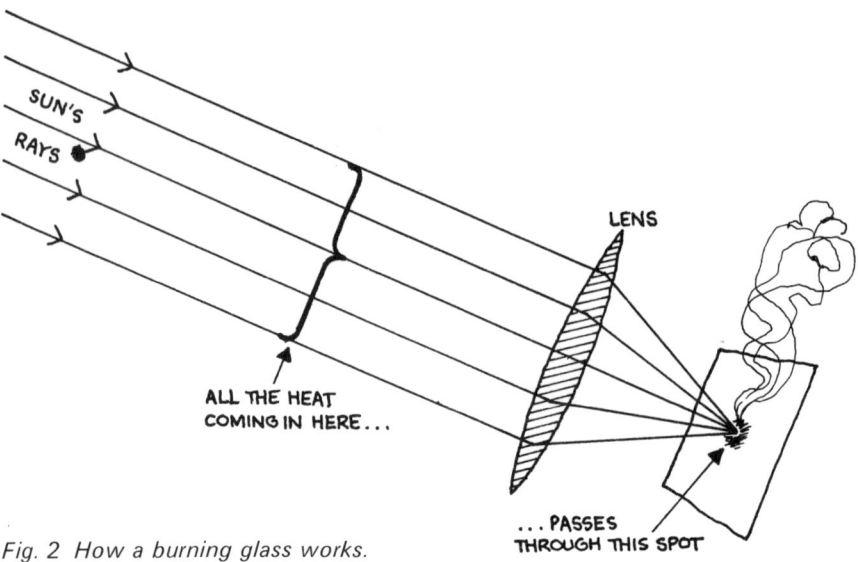

Fig. 2 How a burning glass works.

Experiment 3: On a warm, sunny day use a magnifying glass to focus the sun's rays onto a small spot on a piece of card or paper (Figure 2). You should soon see a wisp of smoke rise from the brilliant light spot and a charred hole appear.

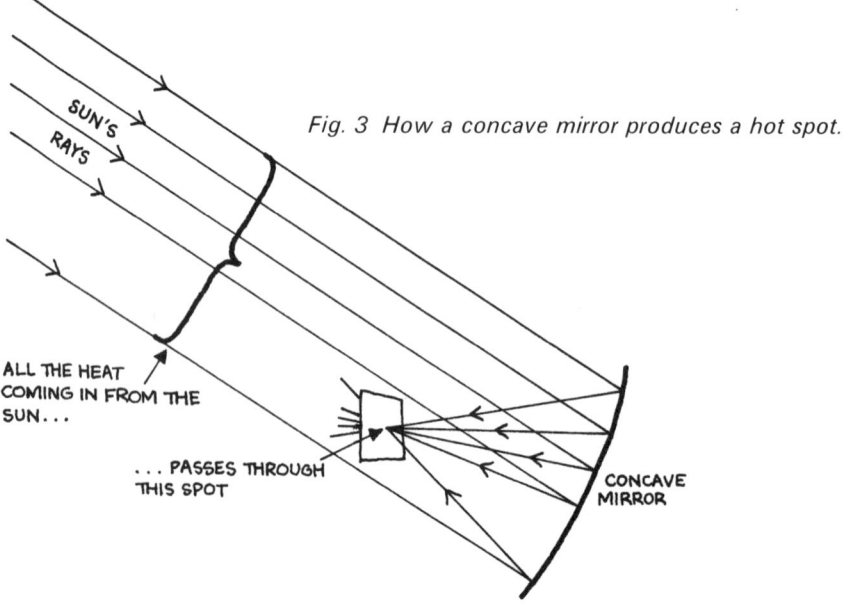

Fig. 3 How a concave mirror produces a hot spot.

Early uses of fire

Next, try borrowing a shaving mirror with a saucer-shaped reflecting surface (concave). Turn it towards the sun and move a piece of card about in front of the mirror until you find where the sun's rays focus (Figure 3). See if you can make it smoulder this time. **Caution: do not try to find the spot of light by looking directly into the mirror; it will damage your eyes.**

The Incas of Peru used a mirror of this sort to light the sacred flame with which they worshipped their god of fire. Archimedes is supposed to have destroyed the Spartan fleet off Syracuse by setting fire to their sails with a battery of mirrors.

Flint and steel

You may have struck sparks on a stone with your spade while digging, or you may have seen the shoes of horses making sparks on a road. Surely, then, a good way of making sparks to light a fire would be to strike stone and steel together? This is a method which was once widely used in Europe and is used still by Eskimos, some North American Indians and by people in parts of Asia and Africa.

Before the Iron Age, iron pyrites, an ore of iron combined with sulphur, was used instead of steel. Old European tinder boxes contained flint, which is a grey or black stone, made of quartz, harder than steel or glass, and found widely in England. They also contained a piece of steel on which to strike the flint, some material called tinder, which would catch fire easily (charred linen was often used) and some wooden splints with a blob of sulphur on the end, to take a flame from the tinder.

Later (about 1700), pistol tinder boxes were developed. These were derived from the flintlock pistol—in fact many real pistols were converted into tinder boxes. When the trigger was pulled, the flint struck a steel plate and produced a spark. This spark ignited a charge of gunpowder which, in turn, lit the tinder. There were also wheel tinder boxes, in which an iron wheel was made to rotate rapidly against a fixed flint. Today the petrol lighter uses the same principle: the grooved wheel is made of steel and the 'flint' is an alloy of zirconium, which sparks readily.

Matches

Matches were first made during the beginning of the nineteenth century. They are different from all other methods of fire-making in that they depend on energy produced in a chemical reaction rather than on heat produced

(opposite)
Getting a light with an early 19th century tinder box (Photograph: The Science Museum, London: Bryant & May collection)

mechanically or by the sun. It would be better to delay describing them until we have found out something about the nature of flames and burning.

BOOKS TO READ

Look up "Fire" and "Firemaking" in encyclopedias, e.g. *Children's Britannica.*

The Science Museum Illustrated Booklets:

Making Fire (wood friction, tinder boxes, matches);

Lighting 1 (early oil lamps, candles);
            2 (gas, mineral oil, electricity);
            3 (miscellaneous developments),
make very instructive and interesting reading. Obtainable from the Science Museum, South Kensington, London, SW7 2DD.

For an imaginative impression of life in prehistoric times, in which the place of fire in family life can be seen, read *The Inheritors,* by William Golding (Faber & Faber, London, 1964).

Chapter 6, "Cones of Fire", *Modern Knowledge, "Earth's Crust",* K. Clayton (Aldus, London, 1966).

Chapter 1, "The Conquest of Fire", *The Elements, Book 2; "Fire",* B. Henry (John Baker, London, 1968).

The First People in the World, G. Ames and R. Wyler (Blackie, 1961).

Man and His Conquests, "The Conquest of Fire" (Burke, London, 1959).

Fire in Your Life, I. Adler (Dennis Dobson, London, 1961).

Ancient Britons, How They Lived, M. Maitland Howard, Henry Hodges and Edward Pyddoke (John Baker, 1969).

The Study Book of Lamps and Candles, The History of Lighting,
Ray Mitchell (Bodley Head, 1959).

PLACES TO VISIT

The Bryant and May Collection of Firemaking Equipment, in the basement of the Science Museum, South Kensington, London, SW7 2DD.

A Collection of primitive firemaking apparatus in the Pitt Rivers Museum, Oxford.

Your own local museum may well have examples of tinder boxes, drill-sticks or fire ploughs: why not go and find out?

2 ANCIENT STORIES AND SUPERSTITIONS

Because fire plays such an important role in our lives and has given men so much power, ancient civilisations believed that fire must have a god of its own. They made up stories about the life and troubles of their fire god and about the way in which fire was first given to man. Here are a few:

AGNI, THE HINDU GOD OF FIRE

The earliest Indian religious writings describe the universe in terms of three domains: heaven, air and earth. Heaven was the true home of the sun and stars and the gods, though the gods appeared also on earth. In particular, Agni, the Hindu god of the sun, lightning and sacrificial fires, spent much of his time here.

People pictured and described the god Agni in terms suggested by the appearance and behaviour of fires. No wonder he had red limbs and gold hair and that he rode a shining chariot drawn by red horses. His parents were the two sticks of a fire drill and he was born again when they were rubbed together. He enjoyed hiding from the other gods, for instance in water, or tall grass, or in a tree.

While burning quietly in the hearth, a fire keeps a home warm and comfortable, but, when out of control, it can destroy the house and kill the people living in it. So Agni was a two-faced god, both good and evil: one face was kind and the other wicked and threatening. Can you think why he was pictured with three legs, seven tongues, seven arms and carrying a bow and arrows?

HEPHAISTOS, THE GREEK GOD OF FIRE

The ancient Greeks called their god of fire 'Hephaistos'. His father was Zeus, ruler of the gods, of men and of nature; his mother was Hera, queen of the gods, goddess of women and protector of marriage. The Greeks portrayed him as a strong, bearded man with an undershirt covering his left shoulder but with his right arm and shoulder bare. He wore an oval cap and carried a smith's hammer and tongs. His left leg was shorter than his right.

Greek vase from the 6th century BC, in the British Museum.
It shows Hephaistos, on the left, casting in his foundry. He is about to open the hole from which the molten metal will flow.
The fuel for his furnace was probably charcoal. This was the only known material capable of producing the high temperatures needed, when men first smelted metals from their ores, over 6,000 years ago.

Although the Greeks shared their belief in Hephaistos with other races in Europe and Africa, it is surprising that they thought of a lame god, since they loved beauty and perfection and shrank from ugliness and deformity. But Hephaistos was said to have been born weak, lame and ugly, and this so upset his mother, Hera, that she threw him out of Olympus (Heaven). Fortunately he fell into the sea near two nymphs. Eurynome and Thetis. They rescued him and looked after him secretly in an underwater cave where he set up a smithy and made all sorts of jewellery and ornaments.

One of the things Hephaistos made was a golden chair fitted with invisible chains which held fast anyone who sat in it, and from which only he could release them. In revenge for the way in which his mother had thrown him out of Olympus, he sent it to her as a present. She sat in it and became trapped. Hera realised that to escape she must somehow bring Hephaistos back to Olympus, so she sent Ares, the god of war, to fetch him, but Hephaistos frightened him away with his flaming torch. Eventually Dionysus, the god of wine, fetched him back by first making him drunk. Hera now made a fuss of Hephaistos and gave him a much finer smithy, so he settled down happily with her.

Zeus and Hera were always quarrelling, behaviour not really in keeping with their positions as important gods. Once, when Zeus was asleep, Hera encouraged the other Olympians to tie him up and move out of reach the thunderbolt which he used to rule them. When he eventually got free, Zeus was so angry that he hung Hera from the sky by a gold bracelet on each wrist and with an anvil fastened to each ankle. Siding with Hera, Hephaistos reproached Zeus for his cruelty, whereupon Zeus angrily threw him out of Olympus for a second time.

This time Hephaistos was less fortunate: he fell for the whole of one day and broke both his legs on landing on the Island of Lemnos in the Aegean Sea. There the inhabitants looked after him till he was pardoned and returned to Olympus. After this mishap he was only able to walk with the aid of two gold maidens which he made for himself.

HESTIA AND VESTA, THE GREEK AND ROMAN GODDESSES OF THE HEARTH

The Greek goddess of the hearth was named Hestia. She was a daughter of Rhea and Cronus (the two youngest Titans) and a sister of Zeus: thus she was Hephaistos' aunt. Her existence, though virtuous, was less colourful than that of Hephaistos. Although wooed by Apollo and Poseidon, she swore by Zeus' head to live unmarried forever. Whereupon Zeus ordered a hearth to be dedicated to her in every home, in many public buildings and in the temples of the gods.

Other peoples had their gods and stories which were similar to those of the Greeks. For instance: Vulcan was the Roman god of fire and furnaces, the equivalent of Hephaistos; and Vesta was the Roman goddess of fire and the domestic hearth, like the Greek Hestia. Her sanctuary stood between two of the seven hills of Rome—the Capitoline and the Palatine. There were no statues of her in her temple: her symbol was an eternal fire tended by priestesses, the Vestal Virgins, who were beaten if the flame went out. They served for thirty years, ten of which were spent in learning their duties and ten in performing them. The last ten they spent teaching new candidates. Afterwards they were freed from their commitments, even to marry if they wished.

Part of a Greek vase painted in about 425 BC. It shows Prometheus bringing fire from heaven in a stalk of giant fennel, and satyrs lighting torches at it. (Photograph Ashmolean Museum)

Ancient stories and superstitions

HOW FIRE WAS GIVEN TO MAN—THE GREEK STORY

The ancient Greeks explained the gift of fire to man from the gods by the intervention of Prometheus.

Prometheus and Epimetheus, whose names mean 'Forethought' and 'Afterthought', were half-gods, the sons of the Titan, Iapetus, and the nymph, Clymene. The gods gave them the task of teaching men architecture, astronomy, mathematics, medicine and other useful arts and sciences. Zeus became afraid of man's increasing powers and would have destroyed them if Prometheus had not pleaded for them.

One day, when gods and men were meeting together, Prometheus tried to deceive Zeus. He cut up a bull which was to be divided between men and gods, separating the meat and entrails from the bones. Then he made two bags from the hide and put the meat and entrails in one, but put the stomach, which no one would want, on top. In the other bag he put the bones but covered them with a tempting layer of fat. On being offered first choice, Zeus chose the bag of bones with the bit of fat on top.

Now, it may be that Zeus was really taken in, though the ruler of the gods should be cleverer than that, or it may be he only pretended to be deceived so he could have an excuse to be angry with Prometheus. Anyhow, he punished Prometheus by withholding fire from men.

Seeing that without fire men would be unable to cook, forge metals or make pottery, Prometheus decided to steal fire from Olympus for them. He managed to get into Olympus with Athene's help, light a torch from the Sun's fiery chariot and carry away a piece of glowing charcoal from his torch, hidden inside a hollow, pithy stalk of fennel. Then he lit a fire on earth and started showing men how to use it.

When he found out, Zeus was both angry that Prometheus had again cheated him and frightened of the progress that men had made. He punished Prometheus by having him chained to a mountain in the Caucasus, where he sent an eagle to tear out his liver each day and eat it. Every night, Prometheus' liver grew again so the painful punishment was repeated the following day. Many years later, Zeus relented and sent Heracles to release him.

To handicap men, Zeus decided to give them women. He ordered Hephaistos to make a woman out of clay, beautiful like a goddess, and he enlisted the other gods' and goddesses' help to make her attractive to men and smooth-talking but artful, deceitful and idle. He called her 'Pandora' (The Gift of All) and gave her, together with a box which he told her she must never open, to Epimetheus. Although he had been warned by Prometheus not to accept gifts from Zeus, Epimetheus fell for Pandora and married her.

Considering the nature she had been given, it was only a matter of time before Pandora opened the box to see what it held, whereupon out flew, like a cloud of insects, all the diseases and evils that plague mankind. Although she slammed the lid shut again, quickly, only Hope was left inside to encourage men in spite of their misfortunes.

PAGAN FIRE FESTIVALS

We all know the story of Guy Fawkes who was captured while trying to blow up king and parliament on the fifth of November, 1605. We have all burned a guy on a bonfire on November the fifth to commemorate the event. However, ceremonial bonfires were lit regularly at this time of year, the beginning of winter, long before Guy Fawkes. Really, our bonfires are probably the last trace in this country of the fire-festivals which used to be common throughout Europe.

The Celts who inhabited North Western Europe used to have two main fire-festivals. One was on Hallowe'en, 31st October (which is not far off the 5th November), to mark the beginning of their New Year. About this time they would bring their cattle into their homes for winter. At Hallowe'en, too, the souls of the dead were supposed to return to enjoy the warmth of the fire and the comfort of their relatives in their old homes. Also about were witches and warlocks riding brooms or tabby cats turned into coal-black steeds. The other Celtic Fire Festival was on the eve of May Day, marking the beginning of summer when the cattle were let out again to eat the fresh grass.

Elsewhere in Europe these fires were commonly lit in the spring (either on the first Sunday in Lent or on the eve of Easter Sunday), at midsummer and at midwinter (Christmas Eve till Twelfth Night). All these fire-festivals showed similarities to each other: often, peasants danced round the fires or leaped over them and raced or walked in procession with blazing torches round fields, orchards or cow sheds; often they drove their cattle through or round them; in many cases they burned effigies, like our guys, on them, or they pretended to burn a living person on them. Although many of these festivals have been taken over and modified by the Christian Church, similar customs were common before the spread of Christianity and spring from some pagan religion. In those early times live animals and even humans were burned as sacrifices on these fires. With these festivals, simple people believed they could improve the growth of their crops and livestock, ensure that they had more children, prevent lightning striking their homes, and avoid blight, mildew, vermin, diseases and witchcraft.

Since witches were thought to be the cause of poor crops, sterility and the other calamities, it may be that primitive people hoped to prevent them by using fires to kill or drive away witches and other evil spirits. Or, possibly, they realised that the fertility and growth of plants depended very much on the sun so they tried to help its rebirth at midwinter by the magic of imitating it with a fire, and then tried to encourage the sun at midsummer with the example of more fires.

BOOKS TO READ

Look up all the gods named in this chapter in encyclopedias.

Stories of Ancient Greece, R. L. Green (Paul Hamlyn, London, 1967).

Tales of the Greek Heroes, R. L. Green; Puffin Book, PS 119.

Adventures of the Greek Heroes, M. M. McLean and A. Wiseman (Ernest Benn, London, 1962).

Chapter 3: "Fire Legends and Fire Worship", in *The Elements, Book 2, "Fire",* B. Henry (John Baker, London, 1968).

3 WHAT IS **BURNING**?

Fire is so useful and, at the same time, so dangerous that people have believed it to be a gift of the gods. But how did the fire-god make his gift work? What really happens when something burns?

Obviously burning has something to do with air since fires flare up in a draught, and die down when air is kept away.

WHAT IS AIR?

Air must be a mixture of gases because we are constantly adding more gases to it. Smoke, fumes and smells are continually pouring into the air from the chimneys of factories and homes, from the exhausts of cars, lorries and planes, and from ventilators and windows: air must contain all of these to some extent. However, well away from chimneys, exhausts and ventilators we might expect air to have a fairly constant composition.

Let us see if we can find out any more about what air is made of and what part it plays in the process of burning, by means of some experiments.

Since fires are dangerous if they get out of control, make sure a grown-up knows what you are doing, and when and where you are doing it.

You will need:
hydrated lime (often used in the garden, so it may be in the shed),
some bottles with well-fitting corks or stoppers,
a jam jar and lid of the sort you prick with a pin before taking the lid off,
a glass basin or bowl,
a candle,
a packet of 'Flex-straw' drinking straws (because they still work when you bend them),
some 1.5 cm ($\frac{5}{8}$ inch) diameter test-tubes (or small medicine bottles, e.g. 'Aspirin' will do),
Plasticine,
a packet of spills,
washing soda crystals,

What is 'burning'? 29

vinegar,
a box of matches,
a bottle of hydrogen peroxide,
and some potassium permanganate crystals.
The last three items should only be used when there is a grown-up present.

You will find a bottle of limewater useful, but since it takes some time
to prepare, make it beforehand, as follows:

Put a tablespoonful of hydrated lime into a clean wine or squash bottle.
Always make sure that you do not get chemicals on your skin.
Run in cold water until the bottle is about three-quarters full. Cork it or
screw on the cap, then shake the bottle vigorously for two or three
minutes, removing the stopper from time to time; this will give some of the
lime a chance to dissolve in the water. Now let the bottle stand until
the liquid is absolutely clear and all the undissolved lime has settled to the
bottom as a sediment. This may take half a day. Slowly and carefully
pour the clear liquid into another bottle, stopping before any cloudy
liquid runs in. Cork or recap this bottle of clear, colourless liquid and
stick on a label saying 'limewater'. A competent chemist always labels his
containers straight away because afterwards they tend to look alike and it is
easy to forget what is in them.

WHAT PART DOES AIR PLAY WHEN A CANDLE BURNS?

Experiment 4: You will need a jam jar and 'push off' lid with a
pinhole in it. Mark off centimetres (or inches) along a narrow strip of
paper and stick it on to the jar with Sellotape, with zero at the bottom
(see Figure 4 (a)).

Put the jam jar lid upside down in the glass bowl containing about
2.5 cm (1 inch) depth of water. Stand the candle on the lid and light it.
Turn the jam jar upside down and lower it quickly round the lighted
candle, so that it rests on the lid at the bottom of the bowl:
see Figure 4 (b).

(1) You noticed that the flame went out? How long was that after
    you put the jar over it?
(2) Did the jar feel warmer at any stage?
(3) You saw the water level rise inside the jar. At what stage did
    the water rise most?
(4) Did you see a faint mist settling on the inside of the jar?

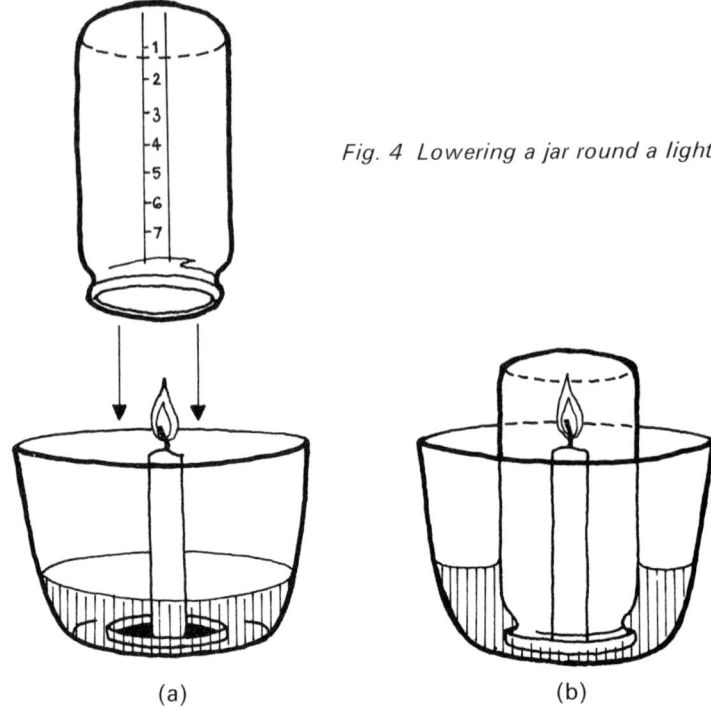

Fig. 4 Lowering a jar round a lighted candle.

(5) How many centimetres (or inches) of 'air-space' were left in the jar at the end of the experiment?

Before we try to explain what happened it would be wise to see if the same things happen every time. So I suggest you try again two or three more times. Make sure you fill the jar with fresh air every time, by filling it with water to push the old air out, then pouring the water out so that fresh air takes its place.

I imagine your findings are like mine:
(1) The candle always burns for about the same length of time.
(2) The jar gets slightly warmer while the flame is burning and cools down after it has gone out.
(3) Water comes in through the pinhole in the lid and the water level rises inside the jar slowly while the candle is burning but rapidly just after it has gone out.
(4) If you started with a dry jar, you may have noticed a faint mist settling on the inside of the jar the first time you did the experiment. (This was water, a substance often formed as a result of burning.)

What is 'burning'? 31

How can we account for what we have found?
Why did the water level rise?
Why did it go on rising for a while after the candle had gone out?
Why did the candle go out?

Water rose in the jar because air was being used up by the burning candle. It carried on rising after the candle had gone out because air or any other gas tries to expand when it gets warm and to shrink when it cools. When the candle went out, the gas left inside the jar cooled and shrank, drawing in still more water so that the level kept on rising for a while.

To see if we can find out why the candle went out let us examine the gas that is left in the jar.

Tests to find out what the gas is like that is left in the jar

To make the gas easier to get at, take the jar out of the water, with its lid on. Then turn it the right way up.
(a) Light a spill, lift the lid very slightly so that you can put the lighted end of the spill well down into the jar, and watch what happens. Unless you have made a draught when putting in the spill, you should find it goes out immediately. In fact none of the common substances that burn will carry on burning inside that jar of gas.

Fig. 5 Collecting a sample of gas from a jar.

(b) Next, we want to collect a sample of the gas in the jar. To do this, fill a test-tube with water (or an 'Aspirin' type bottle if you have no test-tubes). Remove the lid from the jam jar and pour the water from the tube into the jar, putting the mouth of the tube as far down in the jar as possible. The gas taking the water's place in the tube can only come from inside the jar. (See Figure 5.) Remove the tube and cork it (or put your thumb over its mouth) until you are ready. Then pour in a small amount of limewater, shake the tube with the limewater in and note what happens.

Does the limewater turn cloudy white? Does it do the same if you wash out the tube and try again using fresh air? You will find that it does not, providing you first fill the tube with water and then empty it to change the air in it completely.

This means that burning the candle has produced a new gas which, unlike air, turns limewater milky. This gas, also produced when paper, coal, paraffin, petrol and many other substances burn, is called carbon dioxide. Let us call it that, too, without worrying what the name means, for the time being.

Two possible explanations of what we have found are:
either The candle used up all the air, replacing it with carbon dioxide. Then it went out.
or The candle used up the part of the air in which it could burn and then it went out, leaving behind: (i) the part in which it could not burn; and (ii) carbon dioxide.

To help us see if either explanation is the right one, we could remove the carbon dioxide formed when a candle burns and see if any other gas is left.

Is there any gas other than carbon dioxide left when a candle has burned in air?

Experiment 5: Wet hydrated lime absorbs carbon dioxide. You can use it to remove the carbon dioxide made by the candle when it burns.

Put a teaspoonful of hydrated lime into the jam jar and add a small amount of water—sufficient to make it into a thick paste. Now roll the jar so that the paste coats the sides and base. Stand the lighted candle on the upturned jam jar lid in the glass bowl containing water, just as you did in the first experiment, and place the jar upside down over the candle.

What is 'burning'?

As before, water rises inside the jar as air is used up. However, it becomes clear in a few minutes that there will be quite a lot of gas left in the jar when everything has finished; about the same volume as in Experiment 4. If you take out a tubeful of this gas and test it with limewater, as you did in the first experiment, you will find it has no effect at all. Thus, this gas is not carbon dioxide. This gas, in which a candle will not burn and which will not turn limewater milky, is called nitrogen.

Our results fit the second alternative well, though they do not prove it to be correct.

It would help us to accept our second possibility as correct, that air consists of an inactive gas (nitrogen) and an active gas in which a candle (or paper, wood, petrol, etc.) burns, if we could: (1) isolate the active gas in some way; and (2) somehow separate the nitrogen from air, without burning anything.

There is a gas in which things burn very well called oxygen. Let us see what it is like.

Experiment 6: To make and examine some oxygen. This experiment must only be done under grown-up supervision. For this experiment you will need hydrogen peroxide solution and potassium permanganate crystals, both of which can be obtained from the chemist's. Be careful not to spill either of these, and keep them off your hands, skin and eyes. Hydrogen peroxide bleaches materials, and potassium permanganate leaves brown stains.

Roll a piece of Plasticine round one end of a 'Flex-straw' so that you can plug it into a test-tube or aspirin bottle, see Figure 6.

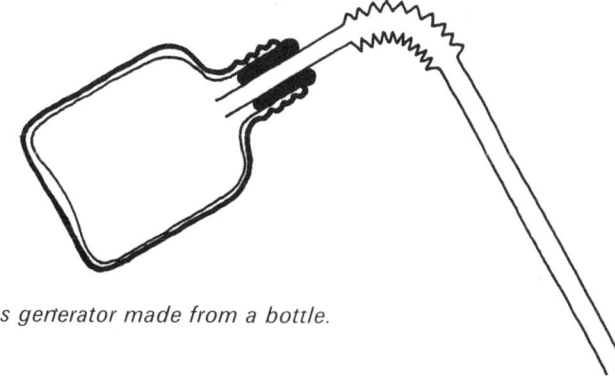

Fig. 6 Gas generator made from a bottle.

Fill a test-tube with water and close its mouth with your thumb. Turn it upside down, put its mouth in a bowl of water and take your thumb away. You should now have a tube upside down and still completely full of water—so it contains no air. One third fill the aspirin bottle with hydrogen peroxide solution. Carefully add four or five potassium permanganate crystals. The frothing shows a gas is being made—this gas is called oxygen. Plug in the 'straw' with Plasticine and collect bubbles of the gas in the tube, as shown in Figure 7.

Fig. 7 Making and collecting a sample of oxygen.

Cork the tube as soon as it is full.

Collect more tubefuls in the same way, corking them and setting them aside till you are ready to test the gas inside.

Light a wooden spill and blow the flame out so that there is a piece of glowing wood at the end. Uncork one of the tubes and put the glowing end inside. The glowing spill bursts into flames and burns more brightly than it did in the open air.

Now pour some limewater in the tube and shake it up. Does it go milky? Try the limewater test on another tube of the gas without putting in a glowing spill. These tests will show you that the burning spill produced carbon dioxide.

What is 'burning'? 35

That spills burn so much more brightly in your fairly pure oxygen agrees with the idea that air is a mixture of oxygen with another gas that does not take part in burning.

Now let us try to obtain nitrogen from the air without burning anything.

Experiment 7: What happens to air when iron rusts? A tuft of steel wool is ideal for this experiment because a small amount has a lot of surface available for rusting. You also, again, need a jam jar with a lid with a pinhole in.

Wet the steel wool thoroughly with water and prop it up inside the upturned jam jar—an old lolly stick will do. Put the lid on and stand the whole set-up in a bowl containing 2-5 cm (1-2 inches) of water for a few days (see Figure 8).

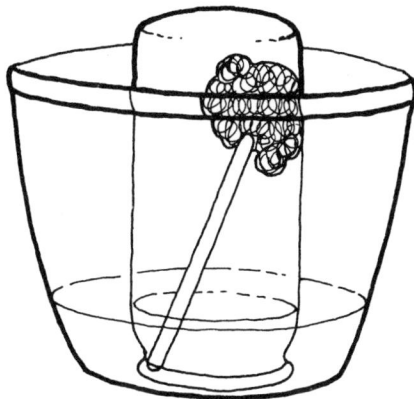

Fig. 8 Steel wool rusting in air inside a jar.

As the steel rusts, the water level goes up inside the jar.
What does that suggest to you?

After a few days, when the water level is steady, gauge, as best you can by eye, what fraction of the air is left ($\frac{1}{2}$, $\frac{2}{3}$, $\frac{3}{4}$, ...?)

Then collect two samples of the gas left in the jar, by lifting the lid, emptying two test tubes of water deep down into the jar and quickly corking the tubes.

Pour some limewater into one tube and shake it.

Put a lighted spill into the other tube.

Is this gas, left after iron rusts, like nitrogen?

We have not proved it, but you now have reasonable grounds for believing me when I say that air is a mixture of mainly two gases: 4 parts of nitrogen to 1 part of oxygen, together with a small proportion of water vapour.

Oxygen is the active part of the air which is needed for burning. When something burns in the air it takes out the oxygen and combines with it to form substances called oxides.

Nitrogen is the inactive part; its main effect is to thin out the oxygen. Things burn much less fiercely in air than they do in pure oxygen.

It is difficult to prove that this explanation of the burning process is correct—that is why it was first found out less than 200 years ago.

BOOKS TO READ

The Ladybird Junior Science book, *Air, Wind and Flight.* Try some of the experiments.

Discovering Science, Book 1, *Air,* and try the Experiment Cards, Series 1, *Air,* D. H. Barratt (Arnold)

4 EARLY IDEAS ABOUT THE NATURE OF FIRE

In the last chapter we found out about the part played by air in burning. This explanation was established about 180 years ago. But, long before that, many people had tried to explain what they saw happening when substances were heated or burned. Here are some of the ideas that developed during this time.

THE FOUR 'ELEMENTS'

There was a great thinker, poet and religious teacher named Empedocles who lived about 2,400 years ago. He thought the universe was made entirely from four fundamental substances or elements, which he called earth, water, air and fire. Three of them, earth, water and air, represented the three common states of matter—solid, liquid and gas. The fourth element, fire, represented the energy which different substances possessed to different degrees. For instance, a great deal of energy in the form of heat is needed to extract metals from their ores and to cast and shape them, and when fuels are burned, surplus energy is given out as the heat and light of flames.

He supposed that all substances were made up from these four components in different proportions. For example, he thought that bones were made of two parts of earth, two parts of water and four parts of fire.

FOUR 'BASIC PROPERTIES' OF MATTER

After Empedocles, Aristotle developed the idea further.

The stream which you get when you boil water seemed to Aristotle to be a sort of air. So he decided that cold water had been changed to air by replacing its cold with hot, i.e. one element had been changed into another by changing one of its basic properties. He thought that there were four basic properties altogether, namely hot, cold, wet and dry, and that each element had two of these properties assigned to it as shown in Figure 9.

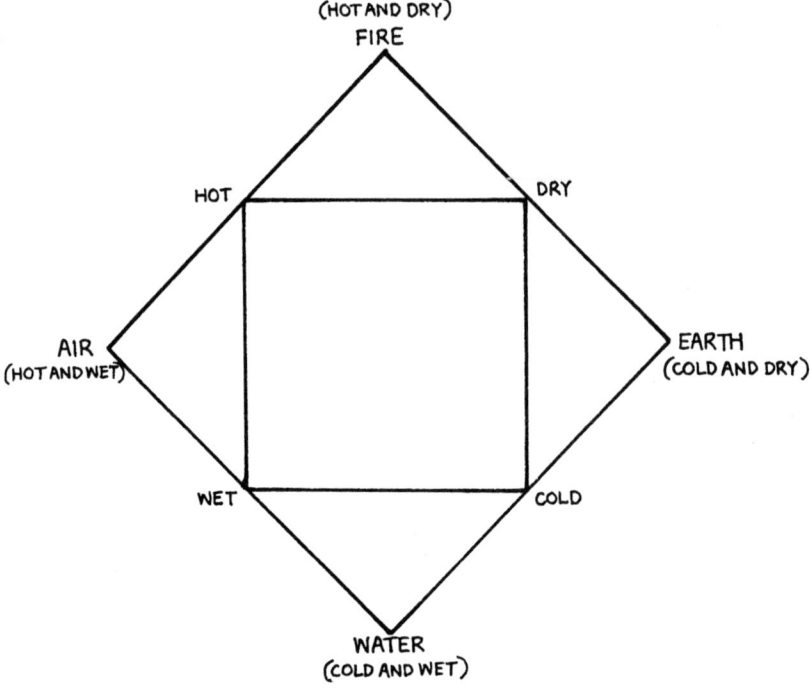

Fig. 9 Relationships between Empedocles' elements and Aristotle's qualities.

ALCHEMY

Though completely false, these ideas seemed good, at the time, to the Greeks and Egyptians in Alexandria. Believing that one element could be turned into another in this sort of way, they tried to turn base metals like lead and iron into the noble metal, gold. Their efforts were carried on by the Arabs who captured Alexandria in AD 640 and had the Greek chemistry books translated into Arabic. The combinations of magic and science which they tried were called 'alchemy', a name which came either from the Greek for fusing and casting a metal, or from the Egyptian for 'Dark Land', which was their name for Egypt. Eventually, alchemy spread to Spain and then through into the rest of medieval Europe.

While some continued vainly trying to change base metals into gold, others, the 'iatrochemists', tried to find a perfect medicine, capable of curing all ills. Here, too, they had no prospect of succeeding.

Early ideas about the nature of fire

Aristotle, Greek Philosopher, 384–322 BC. (Radio Times Hulton Picture Library)

Although the alchemists and iatrochemists could not possibly have achieved their goals, they did a lot of valuable work in investigating the properties of every substance they could find or make. However, scientific progress was greatly handicapped for over two thousand years because of their odd ideas about what matter was like and because they mistakenly believed that fire was a substance like 'earth' or 'water'.

An alchemist's laboratory, about 1650. (The Science Museum, London)

THE PHLOGISTON THEORY

The last and most highly developed version of this belief, that fire was an element, was the phlogiston theory which Professor Georg Ernst Stahl produced in the early part of the eighteenth century.

At that time, many chemists believed that all things were made of air, water and three earths, one of which was a 'fatty earth' which was given off when anything burned. Stahl called this fatty earth 'phlogiston'.

This salamander in a fire is typical of the symbolism which alchemists used to describe their processes. (The Science Museum, London)

When some metals are heated in air, they burn quickly with a brilliant flame and leave a powdery ash. You have seen this for yourself if you have burned a piece of magnesium ribbon. Many other metals do not give a flame on heating but still crumble away to a powder. Alchemists had felt that these processes were all similar and called the powder formed the 'calx' of the metal, and the process 'calcination'.

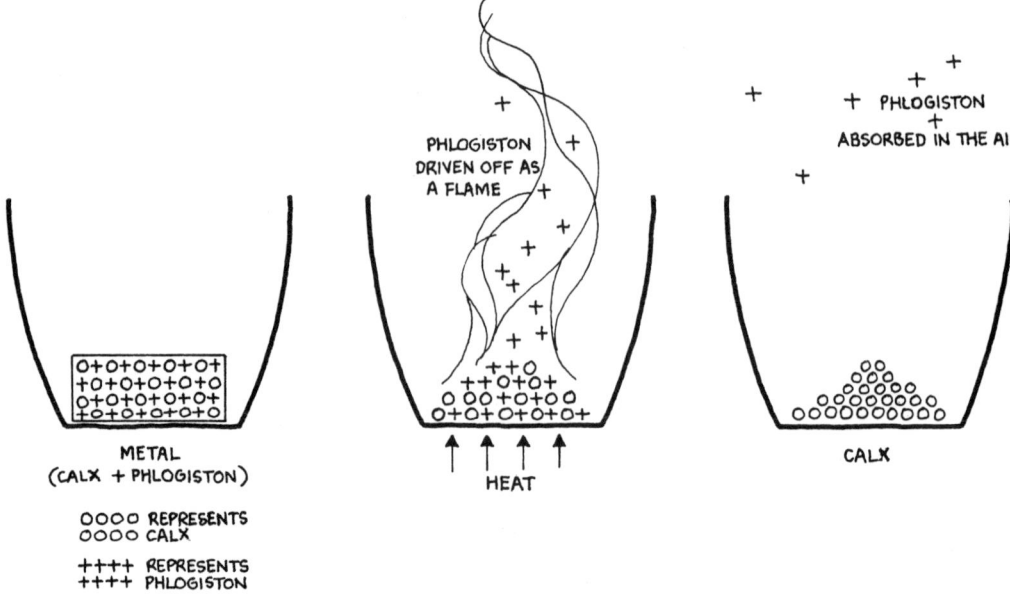

Fig. 10 Effect of heating a metal in air—the phlogiston explanation.

Stahl suggested that a calx was what was left behind when a metal gave up its phlogiston:

metal phlogiston → calx.

He supposed that the only reason air was necessary for burning to take place was because it absorbed the phlogiston and took it away (see Figure 10 for a diagrammatic explanation).

When they heated a calx with charcoal, it changed back to the original metal: this was the way in which they extracted most of their metals from the ores. Stahl explained this by supposing that charcoal was very rich in phlogiston and that it replaced the phlogiston lost by the metal:

calx + phlogiston → metal

(see Figure 11).

If a metal loses phlogiston when it burns, you would expect the calx formed to weigh less than the original metal. During the hundred years leading up to the phlogiston theory, many chemists had found on the

Early ideas about the nature of fire 43

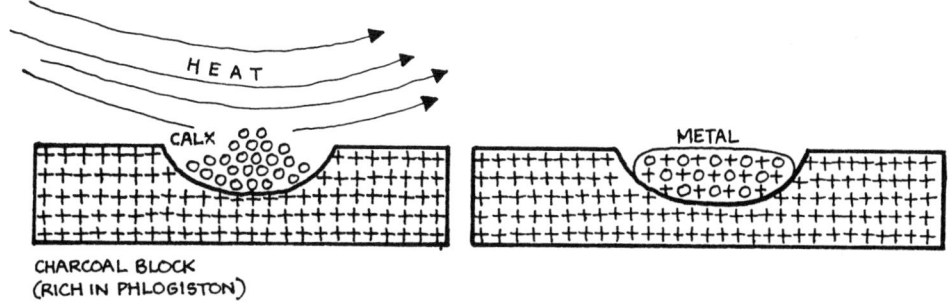

Fig. 11 Heating a calx on a charcoal block—the phlogiston explanation.

contrary that the calxes which they made weighed more than the metal they started with. Now, you and I know why that is. In Chapter 3 we found that a part of the air is taken up when a substance burns (forms its calx). This part of the air, oxygen, adds its weight to the weight of the metal in forming the calx, or 'oxide' of the metal.

Some ignored this gain in weight where a loss would have fitted the phlogiston theory better; and others used clever 'explanations' to make the facts fit the theory. For example, that phlogiston had 'negative weight' so things seemed heavier when they lost the buoyancy of their phlogiston.

THE DISCOVERY OF OXYGEN AND THE DOWNFALL OF THE PHLOGISTON THEORY

Joseph Priestley was an eighteenth-century nonconformist minister who became interested in science. In 1774 he was given a large magnifying glass, 30 cm (12 inches) in diameter. Using it as a burning glass he could direct heat onto a substance simply and neatly, without using a flame. On August 1st that year, he tried to extract 'air' (i.e. a gas) from different substances by putting them in small bulbs filled with mercury and inverted over mercury (see Figure 12).

One of the substances he tried was mercury calx, a red powder made by heating mercury gently for a long time in the air. With the stronger heat from the burning glass it gave off a gas readily. He found that a candle burned much more brightly in this gas than in ordinary air and that a mouse could live twice as long when shut in it as it could when confined in ordinary air. Priestley also got the same gas by heating red lead and litharge.

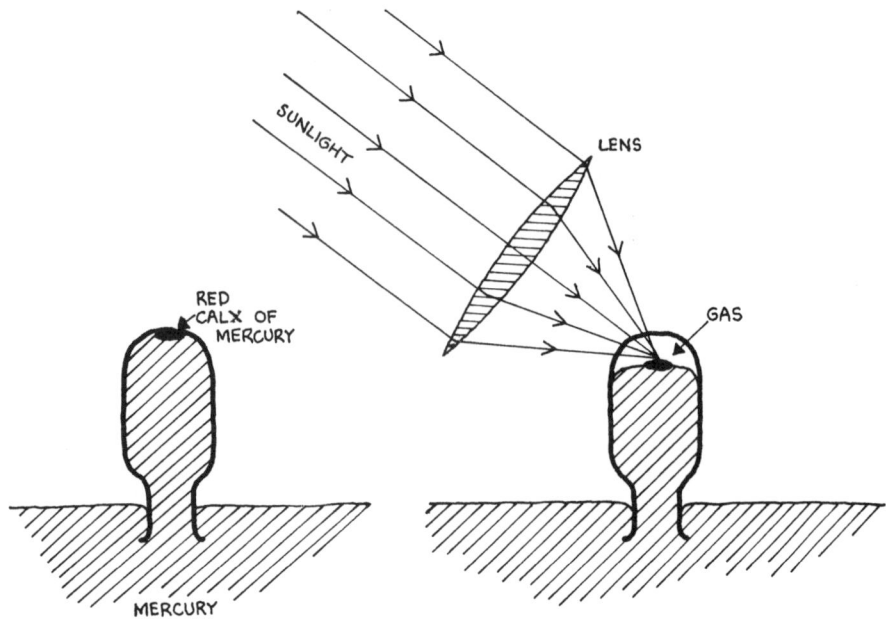

Fig. 12 Priestley's apparatus for extracting an 'air' from mercury calx.

Priestley believed firmly in Stahl's phlogiston theory, according to which air is needed to absorb the phlogiston given off when something burns. He reasoned in terms of this theory that since a candle burned more brightly in the gas from mercury calx, the gas must be even better at absorbing phlogiston than ordinary air is (Priestley thought it was four or five times as good). In other words it contained less phlogiston than air, hence he called the gas he had discovered 'dephlogisticated air'. You are probably thinking that this gas sounds like the one you made from hydrogen peroxide and potassium permanganate, in Chapter 3. And you are right; it was, in fact, oxygen.

M. Antoine Laurent Lavoisier was a brilliant eighteenth-century French scientist who was very interested in exactly what happened to metals when they were calcined (i.e. heated in air till they changed to powder). He was also very keen to find out exactly what part the air played in this. He had found out, as had others before him, that metals gained in weight when calcined and that, in so doing, they absorbed something from the air—but he was at a loss to know what it was. He also knew that when red mercury calx was heated it changed back to metallic mercury,

Early ideas about the nature of fire

Antoine Laurent Lavoisier, French chemist, 1743–1794. (Radio Times Hulton Picture Library)

without using any charcoal. Now this was very surprising to scientists who believed in the phlogiston theory. Where had the phlogiston come from to change the calx to metal?

Then in October 1774, M. and Mme Lavoisier entertained Mr Priestley at dinner in Paris. When Priestley told them about the gas he had collected on heating mercury calx, the Lavoisiers were surprised and interested. This was what Lavoisier was looking for, a gas that combined with metals to make their calxes heavier. The information could have helped him a lot. That it did not is probably due to the fact that Priestley spoke French poorly and Lavoisier understood English badly, and because the dinner table is not a good place for discussing experimental details. It was not until the following February that Lavoisier produced Priestley's gas, by heating red mercury calx. Even then he missed the point. Seeing a candle burned more brightly in this gas than in ordinary air, he thought of it not as the part of the air which supports combustion but merely as a 'purer' form of common air.

Carrying on with his study of air and calcination, Lavoisier gently heated mercury in a retort, A, with 50 cubic inches (820 cm^3) of air confined in A, B and C in the apparatus shown in Figure 13.

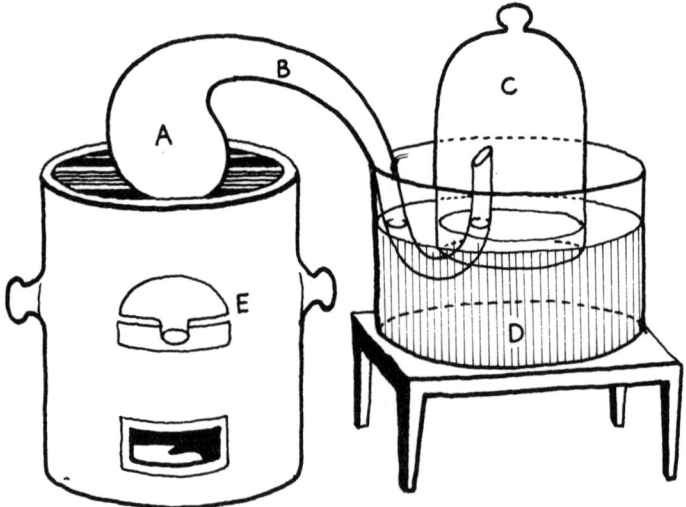

Fig. 13 A, retort; B, neck of retort; C, bell jar in which mercury rises to replace any of the air used up; D, bath of mercury; E, furnace. (Lavoisier's demonstration).

Soon, red specks of mercury calx appeared on the surface of the hot mercury in the retort, A. These increased for four or five days (he kept up the heating for twelve days, altogether). When he allowed the apparatus to cool, Lavoisier found the volume of air had decreased to 42 cubic inches (688 cm^3). He also found that nothing would burn in the 'air' left. This 'air' was the gas we now call nitrogen.

Early ideas about the nature of fire

Next, he collected all the red powder, weighed it and heated it more strongly. He obtained drops of metallic mercury and 8 cubic inches (132 cm^3) of a gas in which things burned much better than in ordinary air. This gas he first called 'vital air' and later he named it 'oxygen'. You notice, of course, that the volume of oxygen produced in the second part of the experiment is equal to the decrease in volume in the first part. Lavoisier found that if he mixed these two gases he obtained a gas just like ordinary air. He also found that the weight of mercury he finished up with was less than the weight of calx he heated.

Try to explain these results in terms of (i) mercury calx being a compound of mercury and a part of the air (oxygen), or (ii) mercury calx being formed by mercury losing phlogiston. I think that you will come to the same conclusion as Lavoisier; that calcination and combustion are both due to combination with oxygen from the air and not to loss of phlogiston.

BOOKS TO READ

Macdonald Illustrated Library 'Science', edited by Dr J. Bronowski (Macdonald, London)
Life Science Library 'Matter', edited by R. E. Lapp and 'Life' editors (Time Life International (Nederland) N.V.), Chapter 1 in particular.
Nuffield Chemistry Background Book, *Burning* (Longman Green and Co., 1967)
Men of Chemistry, K. G. Irwin, Chapters 1 and 2 (Dennis Dobson, London, 1959)

FILM

History of the Discovery of Oxygen, running time 16 minutes, colour. From I.C.I. Film Library. Free loan to schools. Not supplied to private individuals.

PLACES TO VISIT

The Science Museum, South Kensington, London, SW7 2DD. See the display about the Composition of the Atmosphere. Beginning with the Greek idea of elements, it shows how man's ideas of the composition of air developed. Among other things, it shows Priestley's burning glass and collections of apparatus similar to those used by Priestley and Lavoisier. It also contains a lot of other exhibits from pioneer work on the composition of air.

5 FLAMES

SOME EXPERIMENTS WITH FLAMES

You will need:
a candle,
a lump of sugar,
cigarette ash,
a metal milk bottle top,
a clothes peg,
a strip of wood, e.g. an old pencil

Experiment 8: To find out more about flames—what they are and what goes on in them—I should like you to light a candle.
(1) Did it light absolutely straight away or did you have to wait for the wick to catch fire? (Mine always takes a little while to catch fire and I expect yours does too.)
(2) Why does the flame stay just where the wick is and not spread over the whole of the candle?
(3) What do you think is going on in the flame anyway?

Let us try to answer question 3 first. In Chapter 3, we found that a candle took up a part of the air (which we called 'oxygen') when it burned, forming carbon dioxide and water vapour and giving out heat. Fairly obviously, it is in the flame that all this happens.

The candle wax vaporises in the heat of the flame and the flame is simply the region where wax vapour combines with oxygen.

All flames are regions where gases combine, giving out light and heat.

Let us now consider question 2. Wax needs a lot of air in which to burn. The wax that soaks up into the wick rises clear of the pool of molten wax on the top of the candle and can get a much more generous supply of air—enough to burn in. On the other hand the wax in the pool cannot stay alight (see Figure 14).

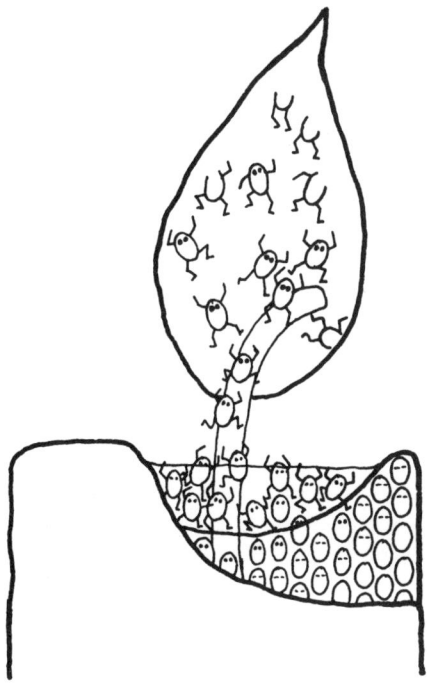

Fig. 14 Molten wax soaking up the wick and burning when it reaches the air.

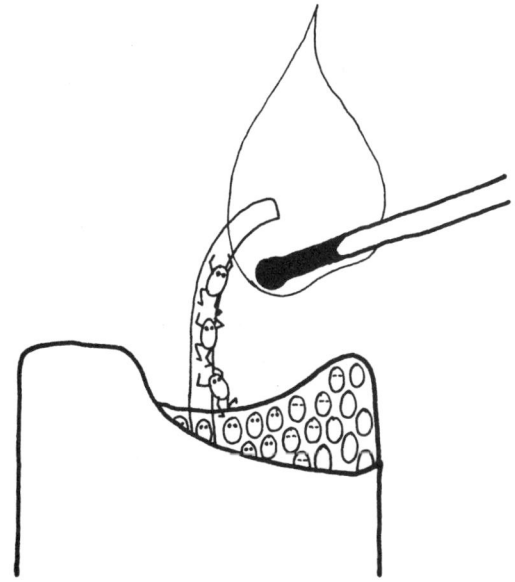

Fig. 15 A candle just about to catch alight.

The answer to question 1 is obvious now. Your candle could not light until some wax had melted, soaked its way up the wick and vaporised (Figure 15).

Experiment 9: Try to light a sugar lump with a match. I imagine you will be no more successful than when I tried.

Now put a little cigarette ash on top of the lump and try again.

Did you have any more success this time? (I generally manage to get a small flame). Here you have another example of a wick helping the vapour of something which only vaporises when hot, to mix with the air and burn.

A cigarette lighter has a wick, too, to help petrol vapour mix with air and burn steadily. Here the difficulty is not in setting fire to the fuel but in preventing it blazing up dangerously. Very volatile, highly flammable petrol is stored inside a metal chamber, out of contact with the air. Its only way to the outside air is up the wick which allows it out sufficiently slowly to burn with a steady flame (Figure 16).

Fig. 16 The wick of a petrol lighter.

Flames 51

Experiment 10: I should like you to take a long, careful look at your candle flame. To see it best, you should darken the room so that the only light is provided by your candle. You will see that the flame is not equally bright all over and some parts are different colours from others. Make a drawing of the flame and colour it. Please do not look at Figure 17 till you have finished yours.

Did you see the bright blue bit at the bottom?—and the almost invisible, faint glow round the outside? You can satisfy yourselves that it is really there, and not just something you imagined, by putting the tip of a paper spill where you think it is. The spill lights quickly.

Fig. 17 Drawing of a candle flame.

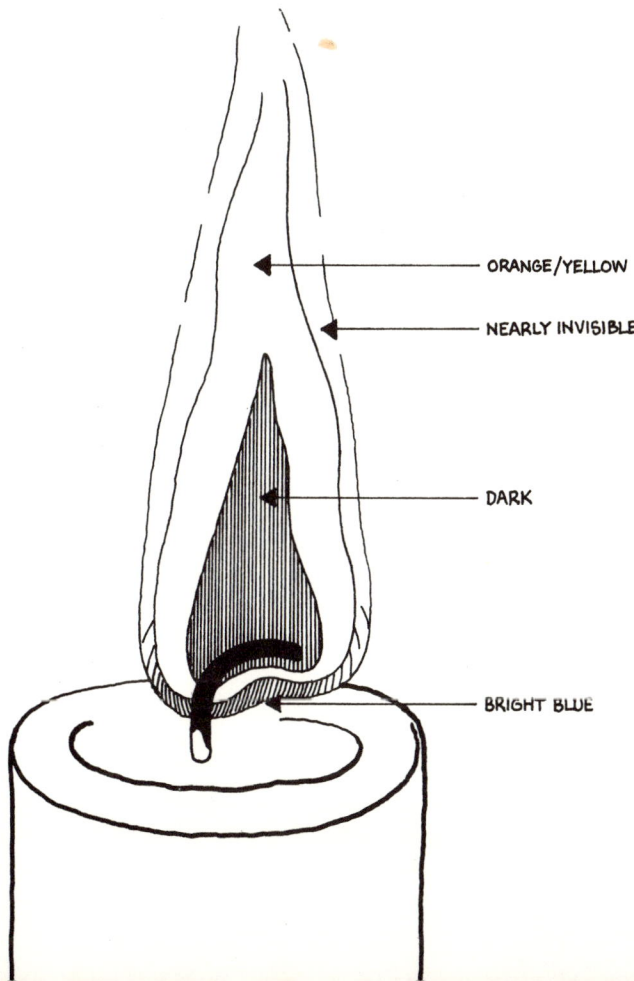

Hold a thin strip of wood (for example a pencil) in the candle flame for a few seconds, so that it passes through the dark patch in the middle of the flame. If you do not leave it in too long, you will find that the wood on either side of the dark part of the flame becomes charred but the bit that was in the dark patch is not marked. What therefore, is the dark part of the flame?

Next, clip a shiny metal milk bottle top into a clothes peg which will serve as a handle. Move the bottle top slowly into the flame (see Figure 18).

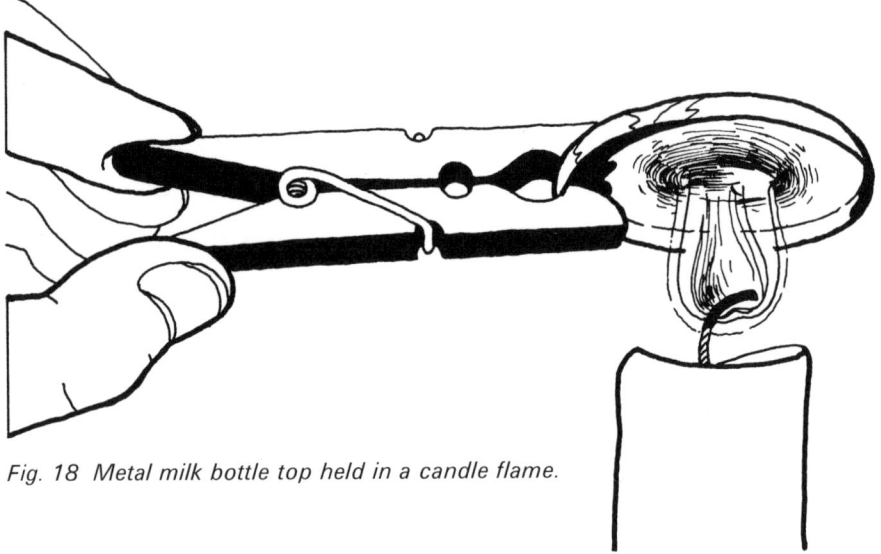

Fig. 18 Metal milk bottle top held in a candle flame.

Apart from getting hot, which is why you must hold it in a clothes peg or something similar, you will find that nothing happens to the milk bottle top until it enters the flame. There it turns dull black.

When the top is cool again, you will find the blackening is due to a thin coating of soot. If you wipe it off, you will find the milk bottle top unchanged underneath.

Soot is an impure form of a simple substance called 'carbon'. Candle wax is made of carbon and hydrogen. In the course of burning, the hydrogen combines with oxygen from the air to form water vapour, and the carbon combines with oxygen to form carbon dioxide. Your milk bottle top was cooling down white-hot carbon particles and collecting them instead of

Flames

leaving them to burn. In fact the bright, pale yellow flame of a candle is due to these millions of minute carbon particles glowing white hot before burning to carbon dioxide.

THE STRUCTURES OF CANDLE WAX, OXYGEN AND SOME OTHER SUBSTANCES

By now you may well be wondering how it is that white candle wax can be made from sooty black carbon and hydrogen—the gas used to fill airships.

There are millions of substances known to chemists (solids, liquids and gases), and it is a big job listing, investigating and classifying them. However, they all turn out to be made from between 90 and 100 simple substances whose properties are well known. These simple substances, which cannot be broken down into simpler ones, are called 'elements' and I shall be calling them that from now on.

In a similar sort of way, there are lots of different types of building in Britain: large houses, small houses, cottages, bungalows, flats, maisonettes, shops, offices, factories, warehouses, laboratories, schools. . . . And there are thousands of different examples of each type. However, they are all made from a small number of different basic building materials: bricks, tiles, glass, girders, beams, planks, sand, cement, pipes, nails, screws and paint.

If you use a microscope to look at a single speck of carbon from the milk bottle top, it looks sufficiently large to be broken up smaller still and yet each piece would still be of carbon. You might wonder if there is a limit to the extent to which you can divide up carbon, or any other element. Lots of people have wondered that in the past. The Greek thinkers, Leucippus and Democritus, suggested, in about 500 BC, that matter was made up of tiny particles, or 'atoms', so small that they could not be split up any further. Since they did not attempt to check their theory by experiment, they do not deserve much credit for being right.

The carbon atoms in your speck of soot are arranged in flat layers one on top of another. Figure 19 shows models of a small part of one layer of carbon atoms.

Each atom is so small that a row of 178,000,000 of them would be about 2.5 cm (1 inch) long. The honeycomb-shaped pattern of atoms continues indefinitely in a sheet.

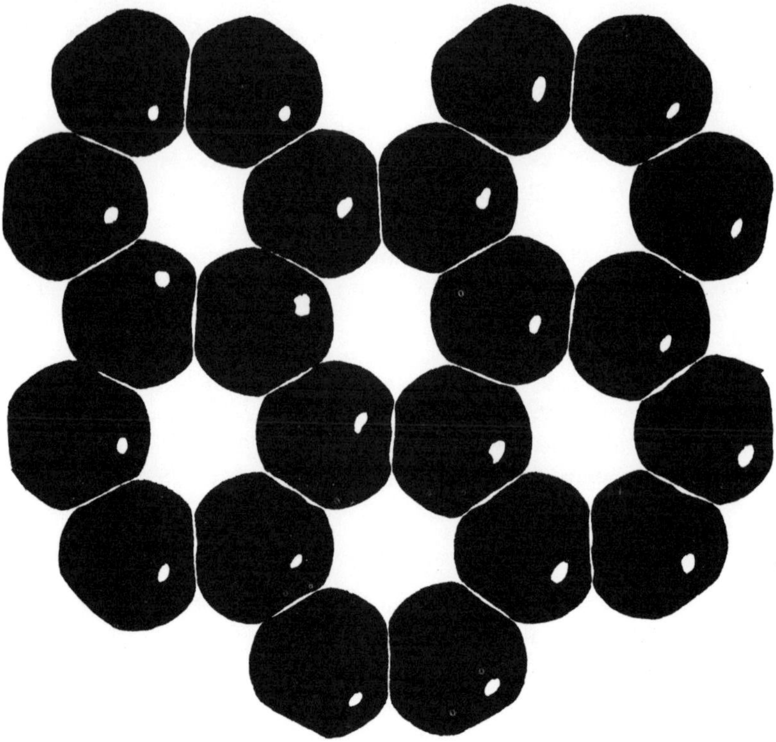

Fig. 19 Model of a small part of a layer of carbon atoms in a speck of soot.

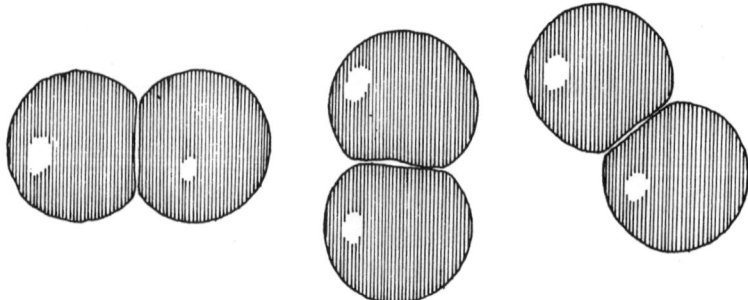

Fig. 20 Models of oxygen molecules.

Flames

The atoms of oxygen gas go about in pairs of atoms joined together as in Figure 20.

Many other substances are made up in similar ways, of lots of small groups of atoms existing independently of each other. A small group of atoms joined together like this is called a molecule.

Figure 21 represents some molecules of carbon dioxide, and molecules of water are shown in Figure 22.

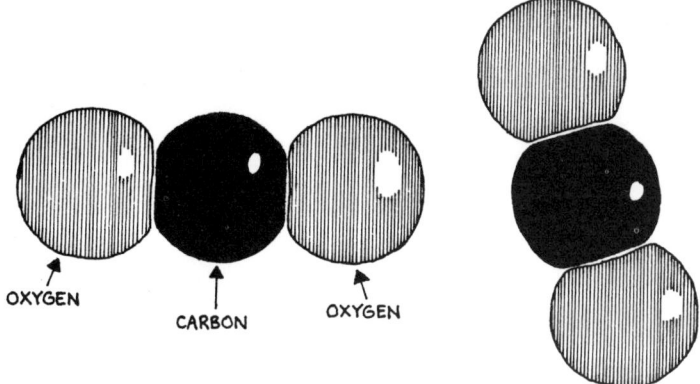

Fig. 21 Models of carbon dioxide molecules.

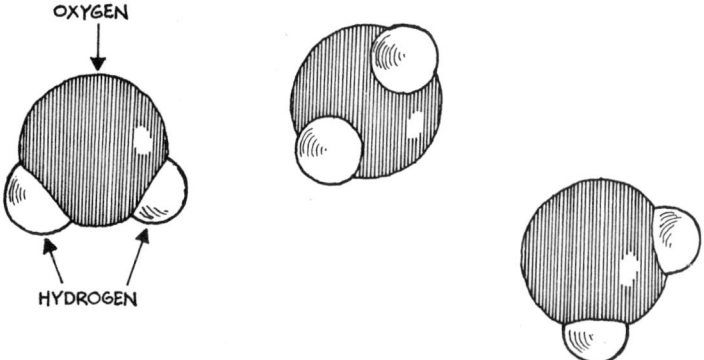

Fig. 22 Models of water molecules.

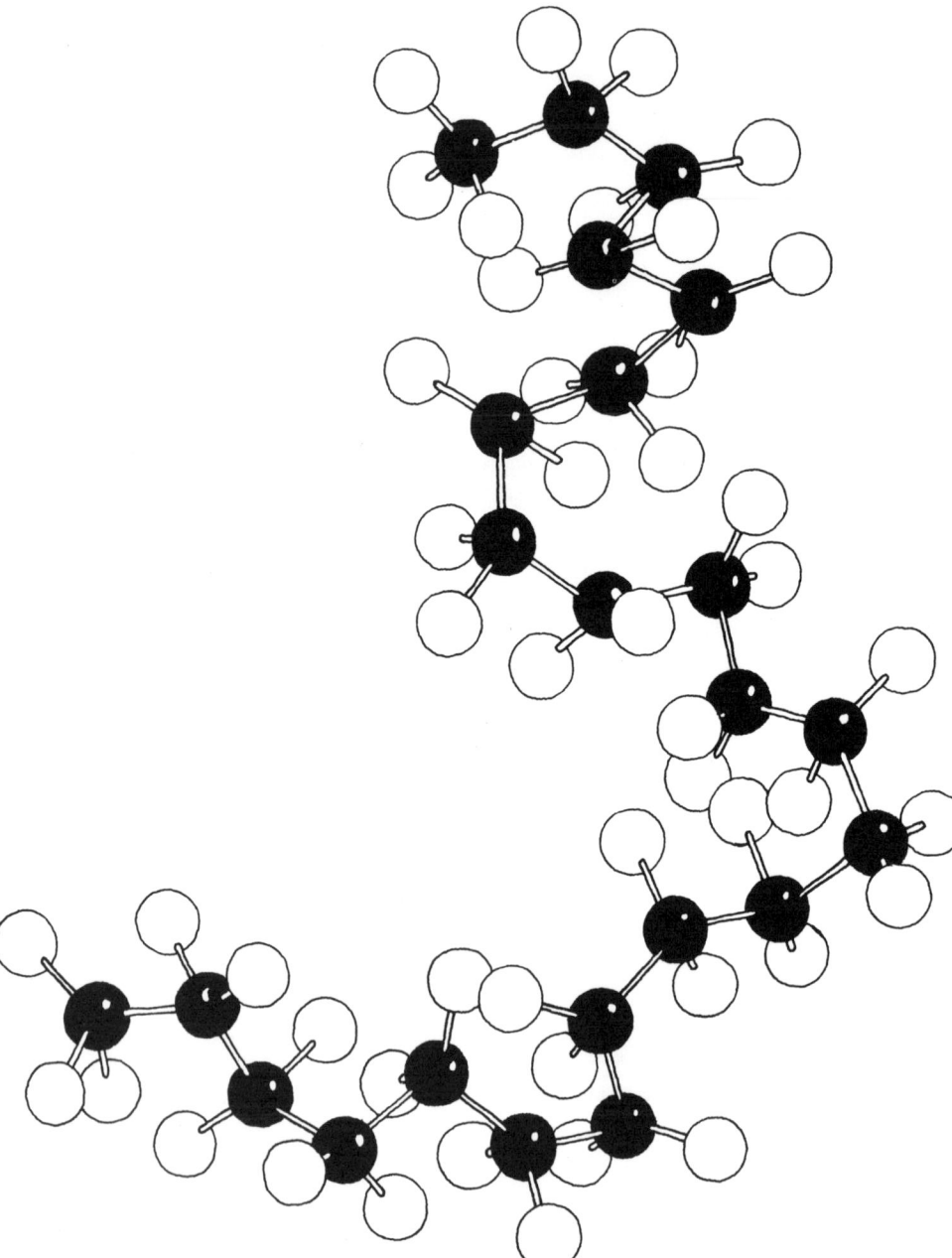

Fig. 23 Model of candle wax molecule, showing the relative positions of carbon and hydrogen atoms.

Flames 57

These two substances, in which the individual molecules each have atoms of different elements joined together in them, are called 'compounds'.

It would be a good idea to get clear in your minds now what the words 'atom', 'molecule', 'element' and 'compound' mean. Then what follows should seem quite straightforward.

Candle wax is a mixture of several compounds of carbon and hydrogen. Each molecule is a long zig-zag chain of carbon atoms (23 to 28 of them) studded with hydrogen atoms. Sometimes the chains are branched. Let us pick out one molecule at random—such as the one shown in Figure 23.

If we straighten it out we can see that it has 23 carbon atoms and 48 hydrogen atoms (see Figure 24).

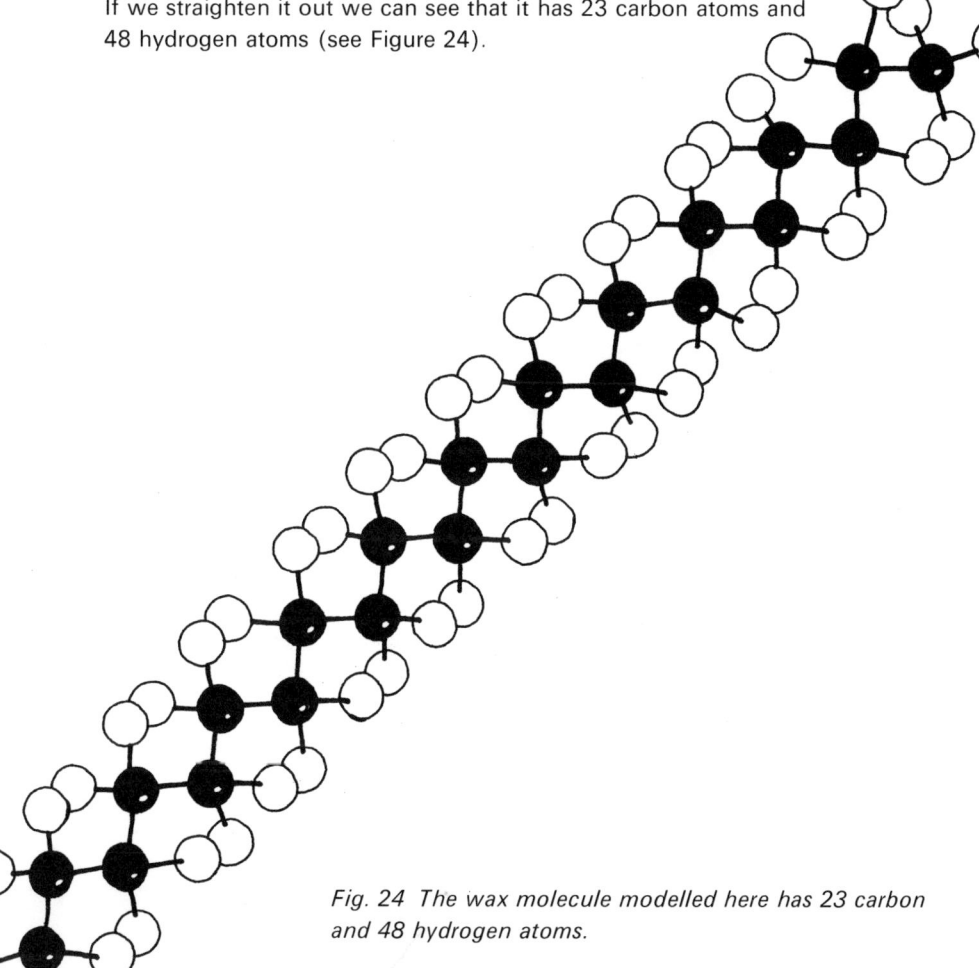

Fig. 24 The wax molecule modelled here has 23 carbon and 48 hydrogen atoms.

HOW DOES WAX BURN?

The dark patch in the middle of the flame contains hot wax vapour which has not started to burn. As the wax vapour gets hotter its molecules break up to form shorter ones, hydrogen and carbon. Perhaps something like those shown in Figure 25.

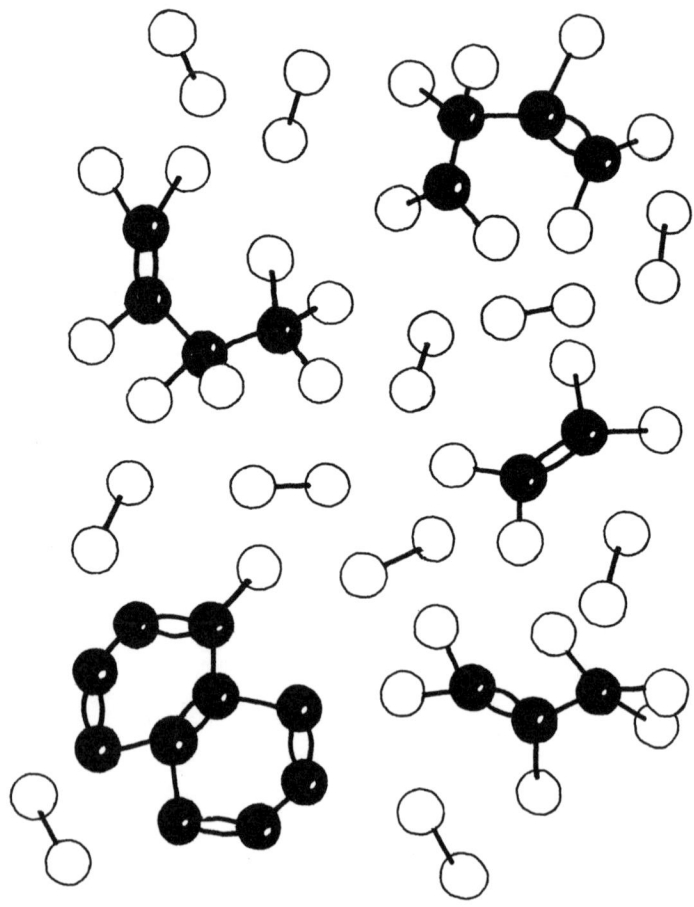

Fig. 25 An idea of what might be formed when a wax molecule breaks up in the heat of a candle flame.

Flames

These molecules begin to burn as they run into oxygen molecules from the air, mixing up with the flame. In the bright yellow region the wax molecules are breaking up into hydrogen and carbon and beginning to burn; remember you found carbon there, because it made a sooty mark on your milk bottle top. The carbon particles glowing white-hot form the luminous, pale yellow part of the flame.

In the nearly invisible, outer part of the flame, the burning is completed and the carbon and hydrogen of the wax are completely converted to carbon dioxide and water vapour. Any carbon particles that escape this region, and cool down, form smoke.

SMOKELESS FUELS

Ordinary coal fires give a lot of smoke because, as they burn, carbon-rich vapours are driven out of the coal more quickly than air can get at them to burn them completely. The solid 'smokeless' fuels you can buy are made from coal by heating it to drive off the more volatile substances, i.e. those that evaporate most easily. This produces a type of coke which will burn freely in an ordinary grate without making smoke.

SOME CHEMICAL ARITHMETIC

Let us work out exactly how many oxygen molecules will be needed to burn, completely, the wax molecule pictured in Figure 24.

First, look at the picture of the oxygen molecules (Figure 20). How many oxygen atoms are there in one oxygen molecule? Now look at the picture of water molecules again (Figure 22). How many hydrogen atoms are joined to one oxygen atom?

How many oxygen atoms will be needed to combine with all 48 hydrogen atoms of our wax molecule?

Therefore, how many oxygen molecules will be needed to combine with this hydrogen?

Now look back at the picture of a carbon dioxide molecule (Figure 21) and work out how many oxygen molecules would be needed to convert all 23 carbon atoms in our molecule of wax to carbon dioxide.

You can now say how many oxygen molecules are needed to burn our wax molecule completely (That's right: $12+23=35$).

You may remember that in Chapter 3 we found only a fifth of the air was oxygen. This means that 35 oxygen molecules are mixed up with another 140 unused molecules, mainly of nitrogen. So our one wax molecule has to get at about 175 assorted molecules in the air in order to burn completely. It is not therefore surprising that it has to take off from the comparatively exposed position near the top of a wick in order to manage it.

A HOT AIR BALLOON

Experiment 11: Why is a candle flame tall and thin, reaching upward from the wick, instead of being a little ball of fire around it?

To find the answer to that one I suggest you make a balloon out of tissue paper and use it as follows:

You can buy tissue paper in sheets, 30 inches × 20 inches (76 cm × 51 cm). You will need:
3 of these sheets of tissue paper,
a pot of paste and a brush,
about a yard (or metre) of thin wire, e.g. fuse wire,
an aluminium milk bottle top.

Take a sheet of wrapping paper or newspaper at least 30 inches (76 cm) long and 10 inches (26 cm) wide. Fold it lengthwise and mark out on it the shape shown in Figure 26.

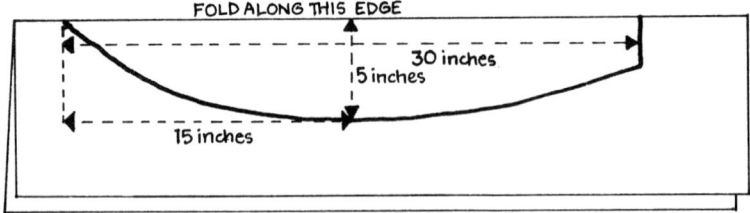

Fig. 26 Template for balloon panels.

Cut it out and unfold it. This is the pattern for each panel of the balloon.

Cut the three sheets of tissue paper in half lengthwise to give you six sheets 30 inches × 10 inches (76 cm × 26 cm). Place these in a neat pile with the paper pattern on top. Cut off the spare tissue that sticks out beyond the edges of the pattern. You should now have six tissue paper panels just like the pattern.

Flames

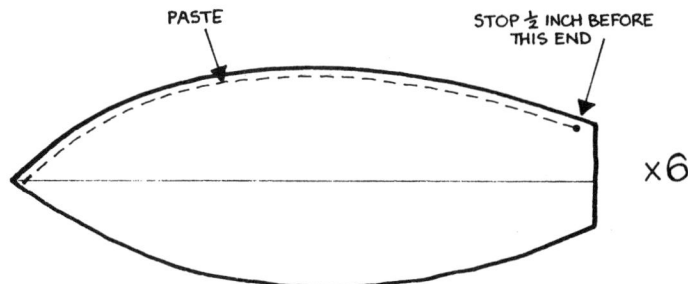

Fig. 27 Pasting a balloon panel.

Lay one panel flat on a hard, washable surface (the kitchen table?). Use a paint brush to put a neat, continuous line of paste all the way down one edge of the panel, where the dotted line shows in Figure 27, and nowhere else.

Then lay a second panel directly on top of the first so that they stick together along the pasted edge. Put the pair of panels aside to dry and join the other panels into two pairs in the same way.

When they have dried, join the pairs of panels together in the same sort of way to make up a six-panelled balloon (Figure 28). Make sure there is no opening left where the points of all six panels meet at the top.

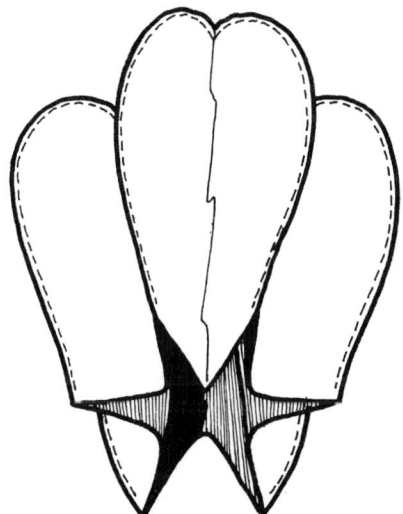

Fig. 28 Balloon made from six tissue panels.

Fire and Fuels

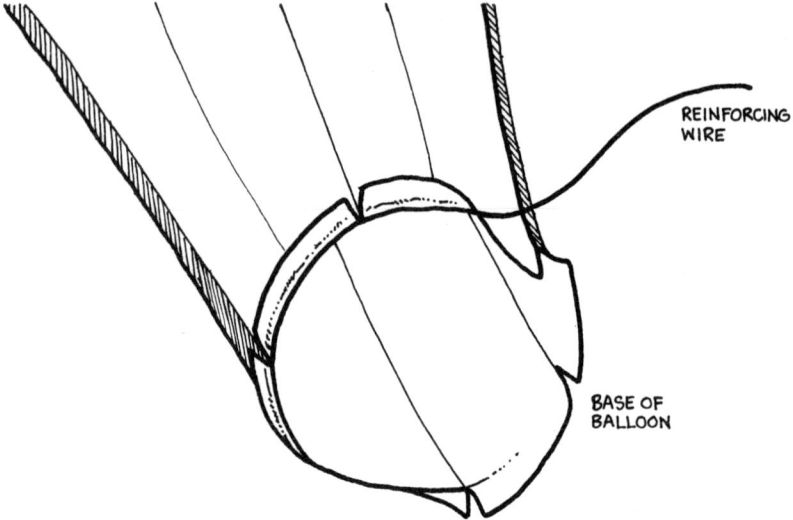

Fig. 29 Strengthening the mouth of the balloon.

Open out the balloon to its inflated shape. Strengthen the hole at the bottom by painting paste along the edge, one panel at a time, and folding the tissue back round a piece of thin wire (e.g. fuse wire) one yard (or a metre) long, so that it forms a hoop (Figure 29).

To fill your balloon with hot air you must get help from a responsible grown-up. This is a job which must be done out of doors because your balloon may catch fire. Choose a calm, dry day.

For a chimney I used a large tin from which I had removed both ends. I clipped three clothes pegs to one end of the tin to form a tripod on which it could stand.

Tips for the adult who has offered to help
(1) As a source of heat I used 'Meta' fuel (obtainable from chemists and commonly used to start barbecue fires).
(2) 'Meta' fuel is **poisonous**; do not leave any pieces where small children can get hold of them.
(3) Four bars of fuel are sufficient. Stack them under the chimney so that the air can get to them easily. Then light them with a match.
(4) Hold the balloon so that its opening is over the chimney (Figure 30). When it is full of hot air—just let go.

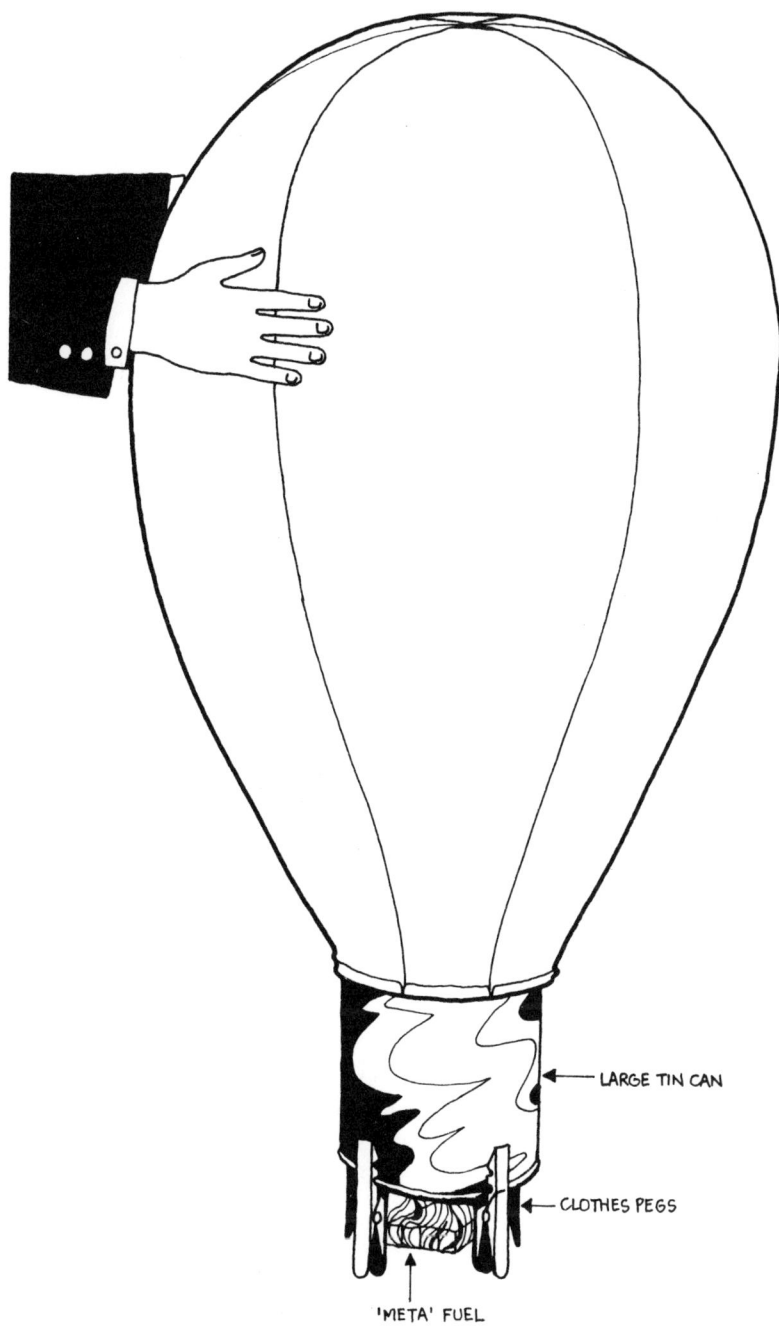

Fig. 30 Filling the balloon with hot air.

If you have made your balloon as I have described, it will go up. If your balloon then turns over and comes down again, it needs a little more weight at the bottom—but not much, otherwise it will not be able to rise.

A neat way of adding the extra weight is to stretch another piece of thin wire across the opening at the bottom of the balloon, with an aluminium milk bottle top threaded on to act as a hearth for a piece of 'Meta' fuel, which the balloon can carry up with it. When the balloon is ready to rise, light the piece of 'Meta' and let it go.

That was fun but do you know why the balloon went up?

The explanation is that when air or any other gas becomes warmer it expands. This means that a balloonful of hot air will weigh less than a balloonful of cold air. So the less dense, hot air rises, carrying the balloon up with it, while the denser cold air sinks to take its place. Since it is the small difference in mass between balloonfuls of hot and cold air that lifts our balloon, we had to be careful not to make our balloon too heavy, else it would not rise at all.

Now, back to our candle flame... You made the balloon to try to find out why candle flames are tall and thin. In and near the flame, the air and the gases produced by burning are very hot; while a little way away the air is colder. As a result the hot light air floats up through the heavier cold air which drops down to take its place. Thus currents of rising and falling air are produced in and near the flame, as shown in Figure 31. They are called 'convection currents'.

Fresh air rushes in and provides plenty of oxygen right down at the base of the flame, so some of the wax vapour burns there very quickly and completely. That is what causes the bright blue, cup-shaped part of the flame. The hot gas produced rises in the heat of the flame, carrying more wax vapour. This vapour breaks up in the heat of the flame, and burns when it mingles with air from just outside. In this way, the whole flame is drawn upwards.

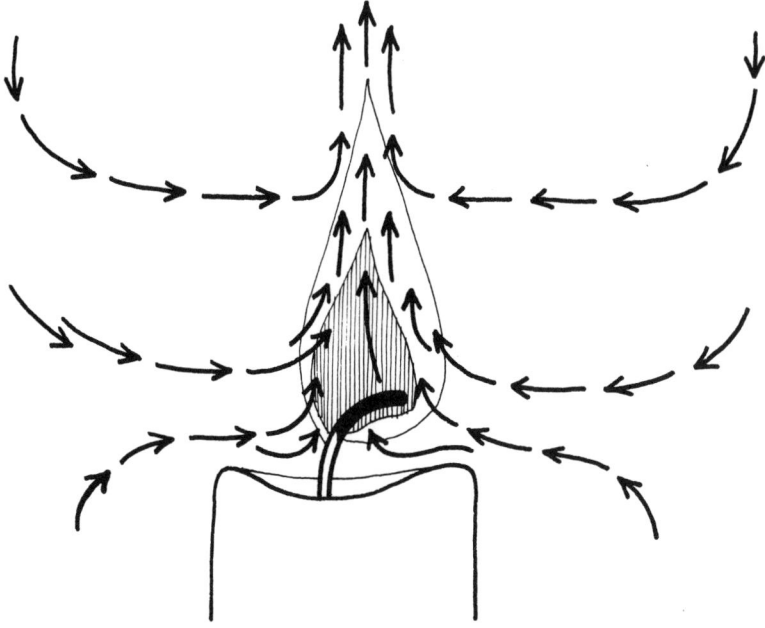

Fig. 31 Convection currents near a candle flame.

6 WHAT HAS ENERGY TO DO WITH BURNING?

Why do we have to light a fire to make it start burning? How does a flame stay alight? Why do fires try to go on burning once they have been started? To answer these questions we must consider things other than fires for a while.

ENERGY

If someone says that you are full of energy, they mean you are able to do a lot of work. Having energy is just that, the ability to do work. If you happen to be doing nothing, your energy is still there as **potential energy;** you are merely not using it. If, as is more likely, you are running about, or playing football or hockey, or carrying home the shopping, you are changing some of your potential energy to movement energy, **kinetic energy.**

You use up energy in working your arms and legs, and when you do, you find you become warm **(heat energy)**. Also you find you grow tired, you are no longer full of energy; you have used up some of your potential energy.

Energy never just disappears. Until you have had a chance to 'let off steam', you are going to be bubbling over with energy. It does not come from nowhere either; sooner or later you have to take in some more energy by having a good meal **(chemical energy)**. What you can do is change energy of one type to another, but finally it always ends up as heat. Your body gets hot, your football or hockey ball becomes a little warmer because you kick or hit it and the pitch warms up slightly through the pounding of your feet. This is why, for instance, snow melts more quickly in towns, where it absorbs heat from the activity of thousands of people, than in the stillness of the heart of the country.

DISORDER

About half an hour after you have started playing in a tidy room at home, do you find you get into trouble because it is in a mess? Have you noticed how difficult and tiring it is to clear everything away when you have finished with it? Do you find it easier to take a clock to bits than to put it together again?

You are not alone in this, the rest of the universe is like you in this respect; everything tends to become untidy or disordered and energy is continually being lost in this way without doing any work. To sort out the muddle and restore order, extra energy always has to be supplied to replace the energy that was wasted.

Now we can begin thinking about the questions at the beginning of this chapter. When your candle burns, the wax and oxygen give up some of their potential energy, which the carbon dioxide and water formed just do not need. This surplus energy is given out in the heat and light of the candle flame. Energy is lost in similar ways in all burning processes. They are 'running down' processes to get rid of unwanted energy—like you 'letting off steam'.

In Chapter 5 there is a picture of a model of a typical wax molecule (Figure 24). They are always long chains of carbon atoms studded with hydrogen atoms; the one in the picture contains twenty-three carbon atoms and forty-eight hydrogen atoms. They are much more neatly arranged in this shaky molecule than they will be after it has burned. Afterwards they are spread out through twenty-three carbon dioxide molecules and twenty-four water molecules, buzzing about at random in the air. Just imagine how unlikely it is that they should ever all come together again to reform a wax molecule. So, in burning, the wax of your candle is also following the natural trend you know so well, that of becoming disordered. All fuels have some sort of order about them which is always lost when they burn.

FLASH POINTS AND IGNITION TEMPERATURES

Why did we have to light our candle with a match before it would burn? If a fuel burns because it has surplus energy and is too tidy, why do fuels not catch fire as soon as they meet the air?

The reason is found in the fact that burning is a process that takes place in stages. Let us return to our candle. We had to melt wax so that it could soak up the wick and then mingle its vapour with the air. This needed heat which the match supplied. If they are to burn with a flame, solid fuels, and the less volatile liquid fuels like paraffin, need heating to turn them into their vapours.

This is not true of the very volatile liquids like lighter fuel, methylated spirit and petrol. Their vapours mix freely with the air at ordinary temperatures, as their smells clearly tell you. The lowest temperature at which a fuel's vapour forms a mixture with the air which can be ignited is called its 'flash point'.

In order to form carbon dioxide molecules containing one carbon atom each, and water molecules containing two hydrogen atoms each, the carbon and hydrogen atoms in a wax molecule must somehow be disconnected from each other. The pairs of atoms which make up oxygen molecules must also be separated, since a water molecule only contains one oxygen atom, and the two oxygen atoms in a carbon dioxide molecule have the carbon atom between them (see the diagrams in Chapter 5). We need a lighted match to start a candle burning, not just to vaporise the wax (reach its flash point) but also to start splitting up the molecules. Similarly, other fuels need some heat to split up molecules and start them burning. The temperature which a fuel must reach to start burning is called its 'ignition temperature', and different fuels have different ignition temperatures.

However, in forming carbon dioxide and water vapour or other products, the atoms give back more heat then we put in. By using this heat to repeat the process with fresh molecules, the flame stays alight and the fuel keeps on burning.

If this is true, we ought to be able to stop a flame burning by taking the heat out of it so that it cannot break up fresh molecules. If you can get some thick copper wire, you could try it this way:

Experiment 12: Wind five or six turns of copper wire round a stout pencil or washing-up mop handle so that, when you slide it off, you have a spiral which you can lower around a candle flame without cutting off the flow of air to the flame (see Figure 32). Since copper is a very good conductor of heat it will carry heat away from the flame, quickly.

If you cannot get stout copper wire, ask a grown-up to make a spiral for you from a wire coat hanger. I advise you not to do this yourself as the other end of the wire whips about a lot, and may well catch your eye.

What has energy to do with burning?

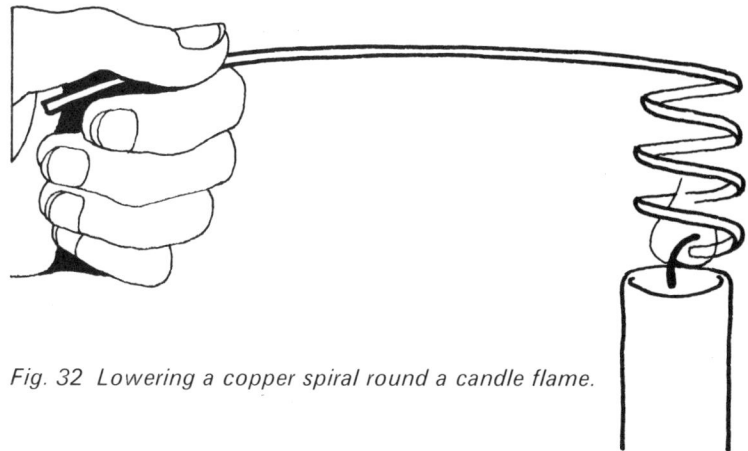

Fig. 32 Lowering a copper spiral round a candle flame.

As you lower the spiral round the candle flame, it should die down and go out. Did the flame die because the spiral was cold, or for some other reason? You can test this by first warming the spiral in the flame and then lowering it slowly. Is there any difference?

MATCHES

When you strike a match, you take advantage of a burning reaction with a low ignition temperature—rubbing the match head against the glasspaper on the side of the box makes it hot enough to catch fire. The easily ignited substances used are red phosphorus, sulphur and compounds of sulphur with phosphorus or antimony. The oxygen, which is also needed, is held in concentrated, solid form in manganese dioxide and potassium chlorate. It breaks free easily from these substances to help burn the phosphorus, sulphur, etc. 'Safety' matches have the oxygen-providing compounds in the match-heads while the red phosphorus is in the glasspaper, thus the match cannot light until these substances are brought together when the match-head is rubbed on the side of the box.

CAN A FIRE START OF ITS OWN ACCORD?

Although fuels do not normally catch fire unless they are ignited in some way, it is possible for a fire to start of its own accord in, for example, a pile of oily rags or dusters soaked in floor polish. The oil or polish starts to combine slowly with the oxygen of whatever air there is within the pile. The heat released, when this happens, cannot escape readily so the temperature inside the heap rises. As more air seeps in, the combination continues and the temperature rises still higher until the heap catches fire. This is called 'spontaneous combustion'.

Have you noticed how hot a heap of damp grass cuttings gets? The dampness in the grass cuttings makes it possible for microscopically small, living creatures called bacteria to break down the large molecules, which make up grass, to form simpler compounds. The bacteria feed on these simpler compounds. As this goes on, a great deal of the energy contained in the original molecules is set free as heat. Therefore the damp grass cuttings become hot.

Hay (thoroughly dried grass) does not rot like this and so it does not get hot. Haystack fires have been blamed on the spontaneous combustion of hay which has not been completely dried. Similarly, fires in hospital blanket stores have been blamed on blankets being put away damp.

BOOKS TO READ

The section entitled 'Heat, the Inevitable Tax on Usefulness' in *Energy*, Life Science Library, Time-Life International (Nederland) N.V.

7 WHEN SPEED IS VITAL

If you find anything in this chapter hard to understand, do not worry—just leave it. However, if you would like to find out more about petrol engines, jets and rockets, there should be something useful for you here.

The energy locked in a fuel is set free when it burns. If you need the energy from a fuel very quickly, you must find a way to burn your fuel very quickly. This means you must mix your fuel with a generous supply of oxygen, beforehand. Let us look at some ways in which this is done.

INTERNAL COMBUSTION ENGINES

Petrol engines

Like candle wax, petrol is also a compound of carbon and hydrogen. Its molecules are smaller than those of candle wax and generally contain eight atoms of carbon and eighteen of hydrogen. The common way of mixing the petrol vapour and air needed in a petrol engine is to squirt a fine spray of petrol into the air as it is being sucked into the engine; that is the job of the carburettor. However, there are some cars, particularly racing cars, in which the petrol is sprayed directly into the cylinders: this is called 'fuel injection'. On igniting the petrol vapour with a spark, it burns very quickly in the air inside the cylinders of a car engine. The hot gases produced expand by pushing the pistons down. The crankshaft changes the up-and-down movement of the pistons into a rotating movement which is passed through the gearbox to the driving wheels of the car. Figure 33 explains how the engine works in more detail.

The cycle then repeats itself over and over again. When a petrol engine is running steadily, there are about forty explosions per second in each cylinder.

Diesel engines

In Chapter 1, we found that air becomes warmer if we compress it suddenly, and that primitive people used this principle in fire pistons as a means of lighting fires. You need go no further than the nearest main road to find the same principle used today by highly civilised people—in

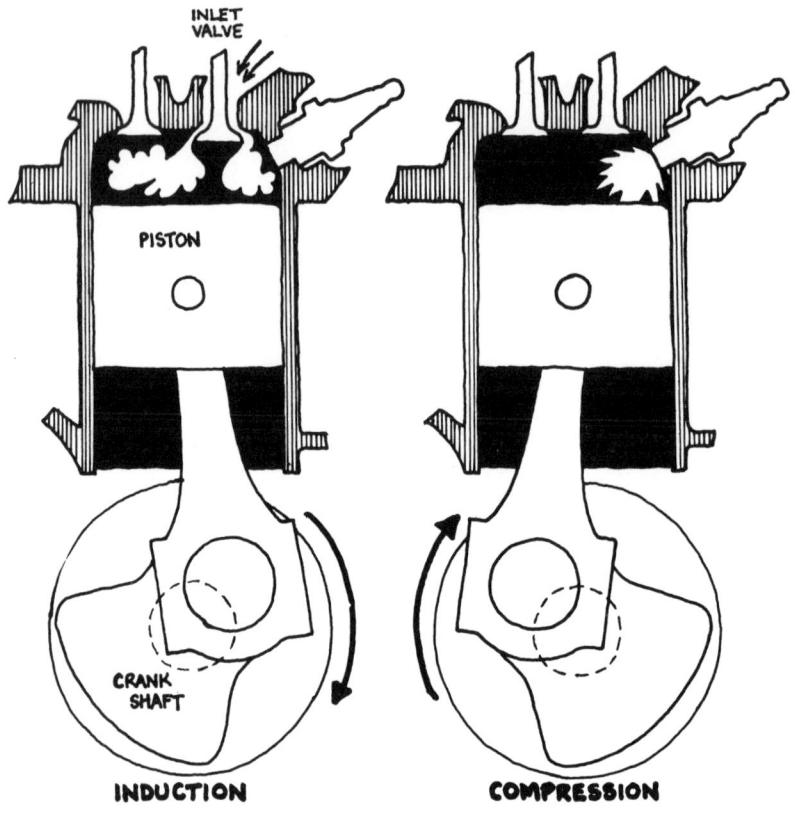

Fig. 33 The four-stroke petrol cycle.
Induction: inlet valve opens, petrol and air sucked in as the piston descends.
Compression: valves close, piston rises and compresses mixture.

When speed is vital 73

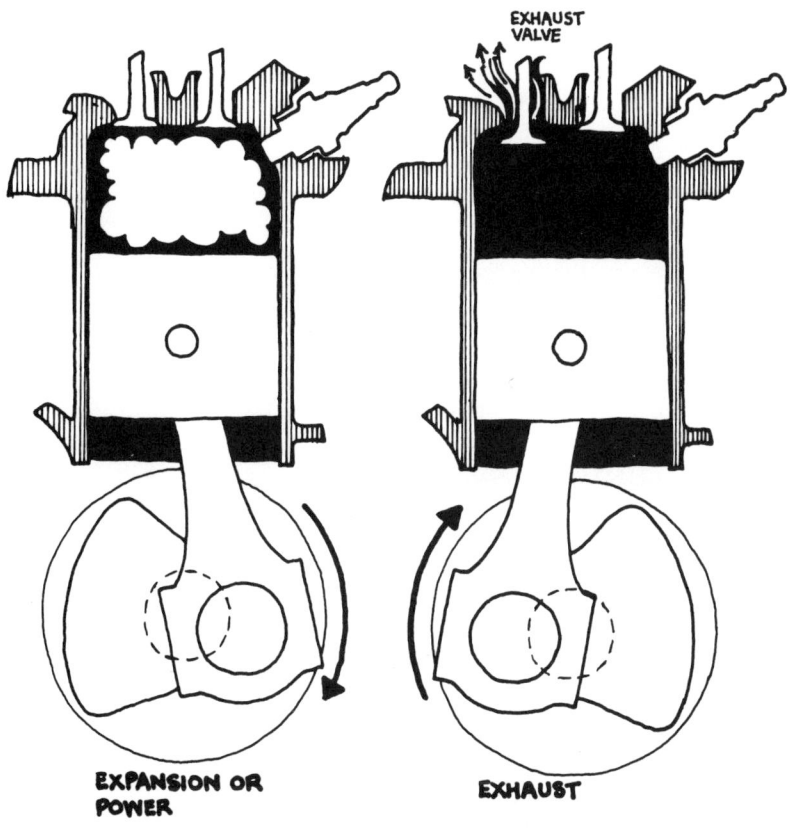

Expansion or power: valves still closed, spark explodes mixture and the piston is driven down.
Exhaust: exhaust valve opens, rising piston pushes the waste gas out.

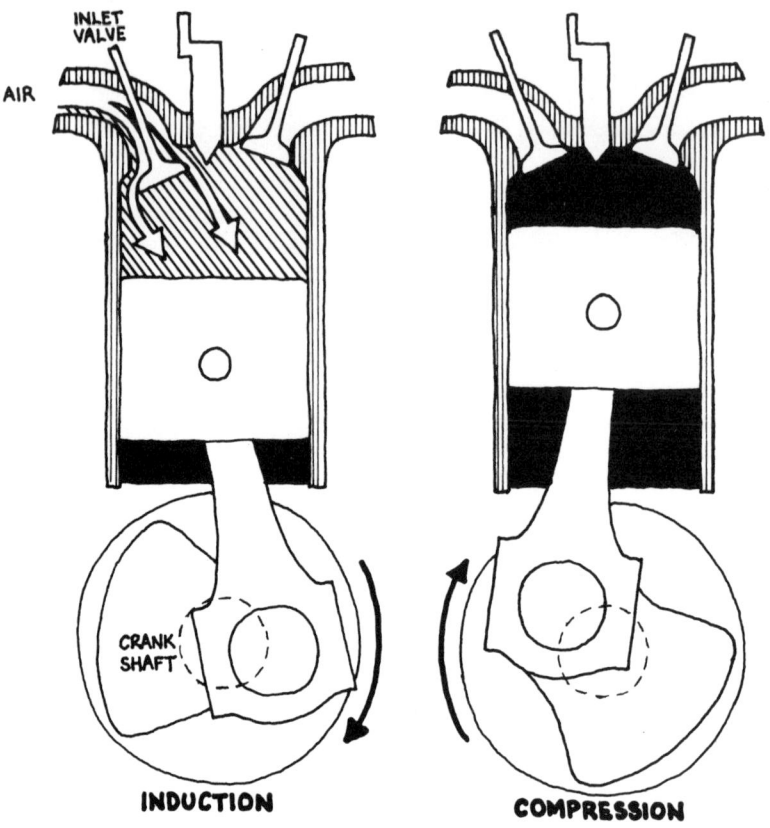

Fig. 34 The four-stroke diesel cycle.
Induction: inlet valve opens, air is sucked in as piston descends.
Compression: valves close, piston rises and compresses air.

diesel engines. In this type of engine only air is taken in by the hot engine during the inlet stroke. The air becomes hotter as the piston rises again and compresses it (see Figure 34).

At the top of the compression stroke, some oil is squirted into the cylinder. Since the temperature in the cylinder is, by now, higher than the ignition temperature of the fuel oil, the oil burns very quickly and drives the piston down again.

Diesel engines run more slowly than petrol engines; when one is running steadily, there may be about twenty-five explosions per second in each cylinder.

When speed is vital   75

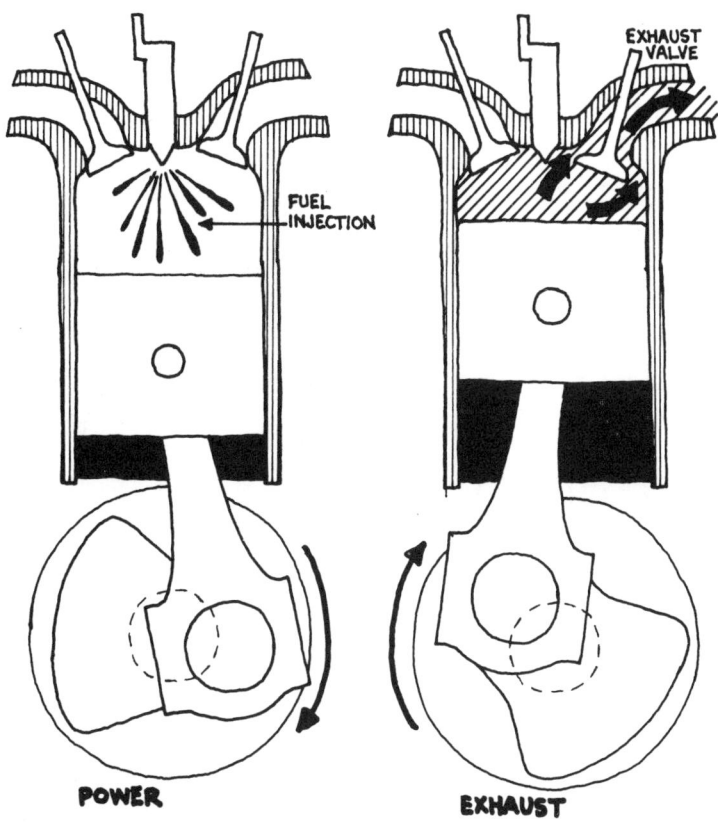

Power: valves still closed, fuel is injected and explodes because the compressed air is hotter than the ignition temperature of the fuel, piston is driven down.
Exhaust: exhaust valve opens, rising piston pushes waste gas out.

Cooling problems

Unfortunately, not all the heat produced in these engines can be made to do useful work. The wasted heat makes the engine hot. Without a cooling system the engine would get hotter and hotter until it damaged itself. That is why air-cooled engines of motor cycles have metal fins round the cylinder to transfer heat as quickly as possible to the air flowing past. Water circulates in the casing of larger engines to carry the unused heat away to a radiator. There, the water gives up its heat to metal fins or a 'honeycomb', kept cool by an air draught drawn through by a fan (see Figure 35).

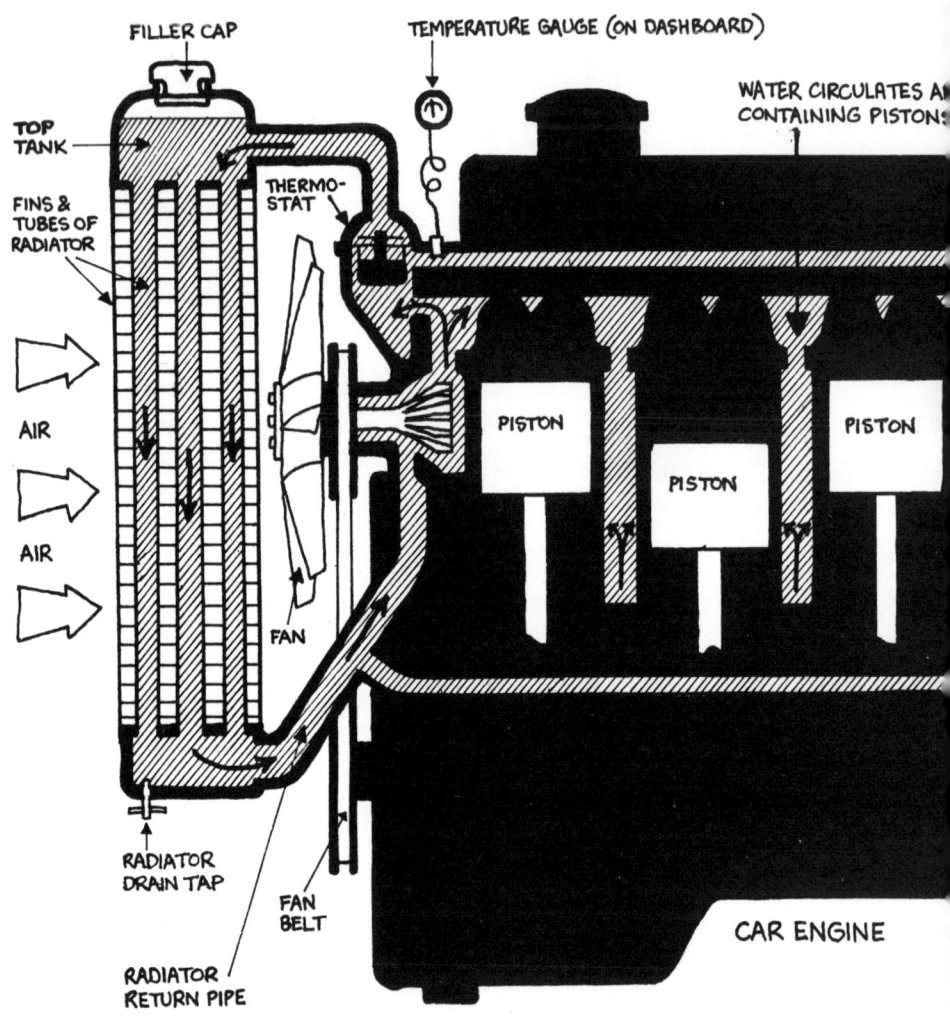

Fig. 35 Water cooling system of an internal combustion engine.

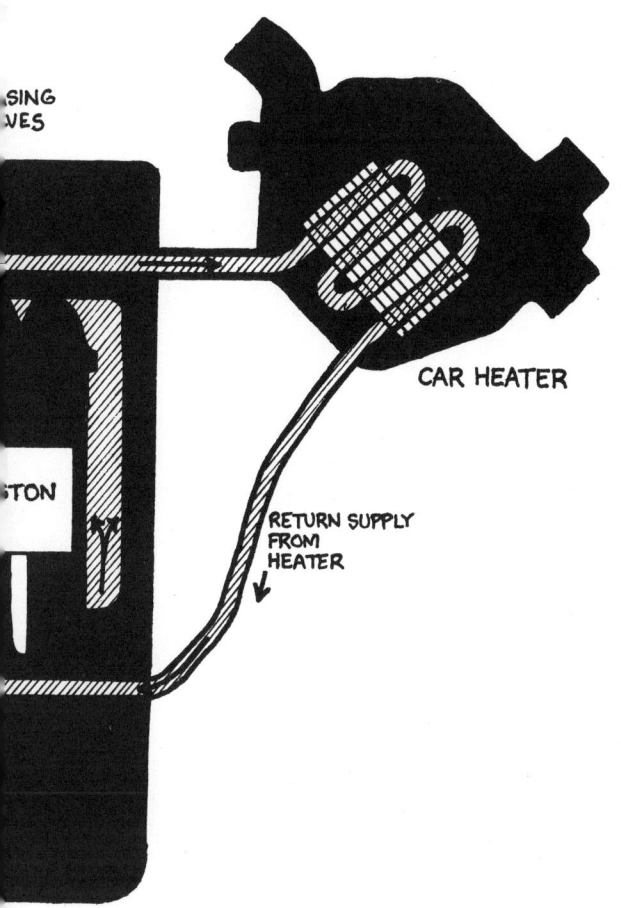

TURBINES

In both of the engines described so far, energy released by burning a fuel drives a piston back. Much energy is wasted in changing this backwards-and-forwards movement into a rotation, which is passed on through gears to drive the wheels or other machinery. This loss of energy can be avoided by using the thrust of the expanding hot gases directly.

As an example let us look at turbines. A gas turbine is a big fan, mounted on a shaft. Hot gases from the burning fuel blow through the fan, turning it like a windmill. The shaft turned by the fan can drive an electricity generator or work other machinery.

A set of fan blades for a steam turbine being built at a power station
(Courtesy of the Central Electricity Generating Board)

In a steam turbine the burning fuel boils water to produce steam at very high pressure. The steam is then blown through the fan with the same effect as in a gas turbine.

Turbo-jet engines
In this type of engine the main thrust of the exhaust blast is used directly to drive the engine forward, together with the aircraft to which

it is fixed. Only a small part of the energy is used to turn the blades of the turbine. This works a compressor at the front of the engine, which sucks in and compresses the air in which the fuel burns inside the engine. Figure 36 shows the layout of a turbo-jet engine.

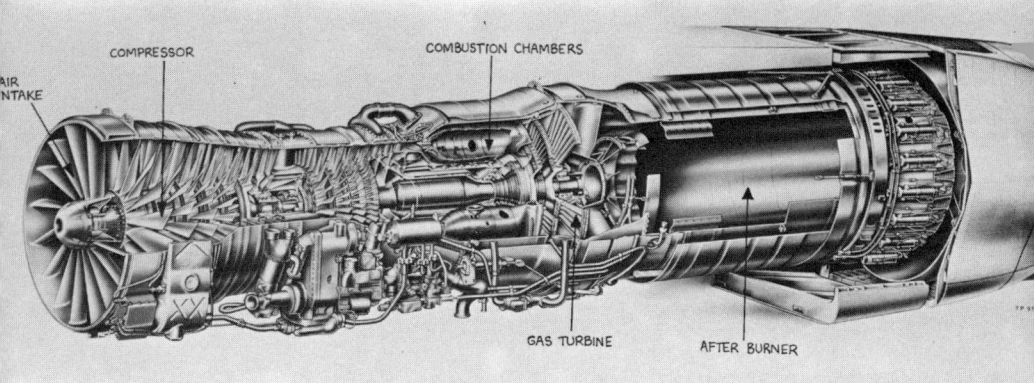

Fig. 36 Olympus 593 Propulsion Unit, four of which power the Concorde *(Courtesy of Rolls-Royce Ltd, Bristol Engine Division)*

Concorde 002, the second Anglo/French supersonic airliner prototype, on the engine running base at the B.A.C.'s Filton airfield. (British Aircraft Corporation (Operating) Ltd., Filton Division)

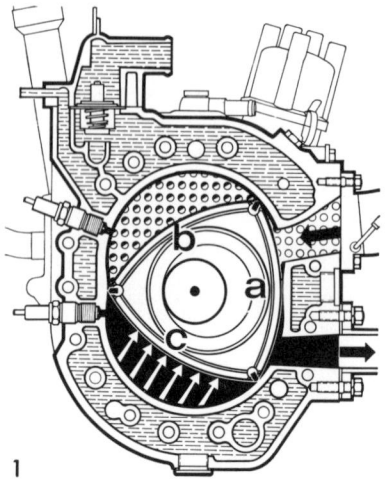 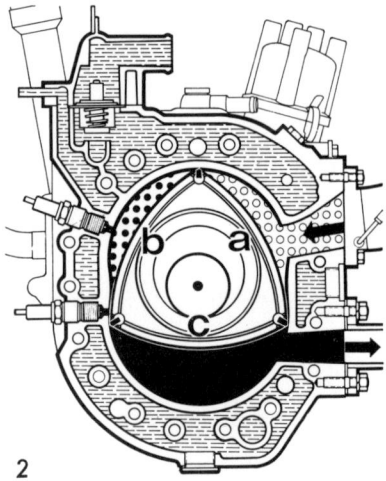

1 Chamber a is at its smallest, denoting the end of the exhaust phase and the beginning of induction. Chamber b is being compressed. Chamber c is expanding after combustion.

2 Chamber a continues to grow larger, induction continues. Chamber b is being further compressed. Chamber c has reached its maximum volume, i.e. end of the expansion phase, and the exhaust port is uncovered.

Fig. 37 The Wankel engine cycle.

ROTARY COMBUSTION ENGINES

Another way of changing energy released by burning directly into rotational energy occurs in the 'rotary combustion engine'. This was first introduced by Felix Wankel in 1954. It works on the same principle as the petrol engine described earlier, but has no valves or pistons.

A triangular piece of metal, called a **rotor,** fits inside a casing so that it forms three chambers. The rotor is made to spin in such a way that the three chambers keep growing larger and then smaller again. The chambers in a rotary combustion engine do the same job as the cylinders in a piston engine. To understand how it works, look at Figure 37, which describes all that happens while the rotor is doing one third of a revolution.

When speed is vital

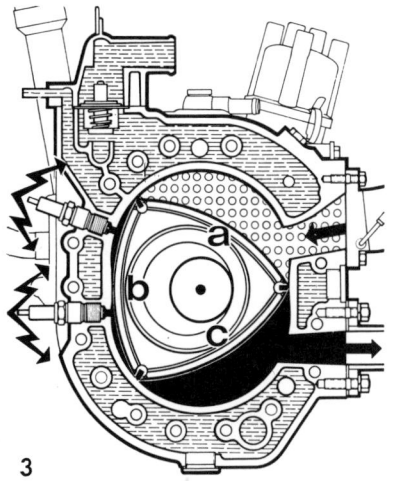

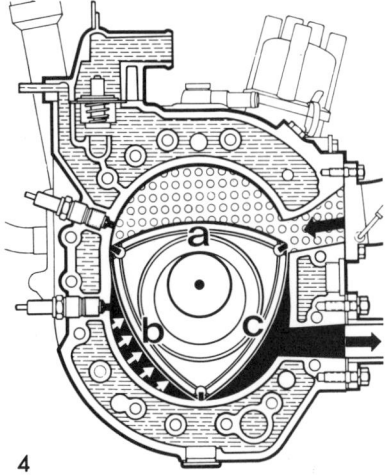

3

Chamber a continues to grow larger, as induction continues. Chamber b is at its smallest, maximum compression has taken place, and the mixture is or will be ignited. Chamber c is growing smaller as the exhaust gases escape through the port.

4

Chamber a has approached its maximum volume, the inlet port is about to be closed. Chamber b, expansion phase in progress, gas pressure acting on the rotor flank turns the eccentric shaft. Chamber c, exhaust phase in progress.

INDUCTION

COMPRESSION

EXPANSION

EXHAUST

ROCKETS

All of the engines I have described so far take in oxygen from the air, which is all right provided you are content to move and work in the atmosphere. In outer space there is no air, so an engine working there has to carry its own supply of oxygen as well as fuel. This is just what a rocket does. The combined load of fuel and oxygen is called the **propellant.** To get as much oxygen into as small a space as possible, space rockets are loaded with liquid oxygen.

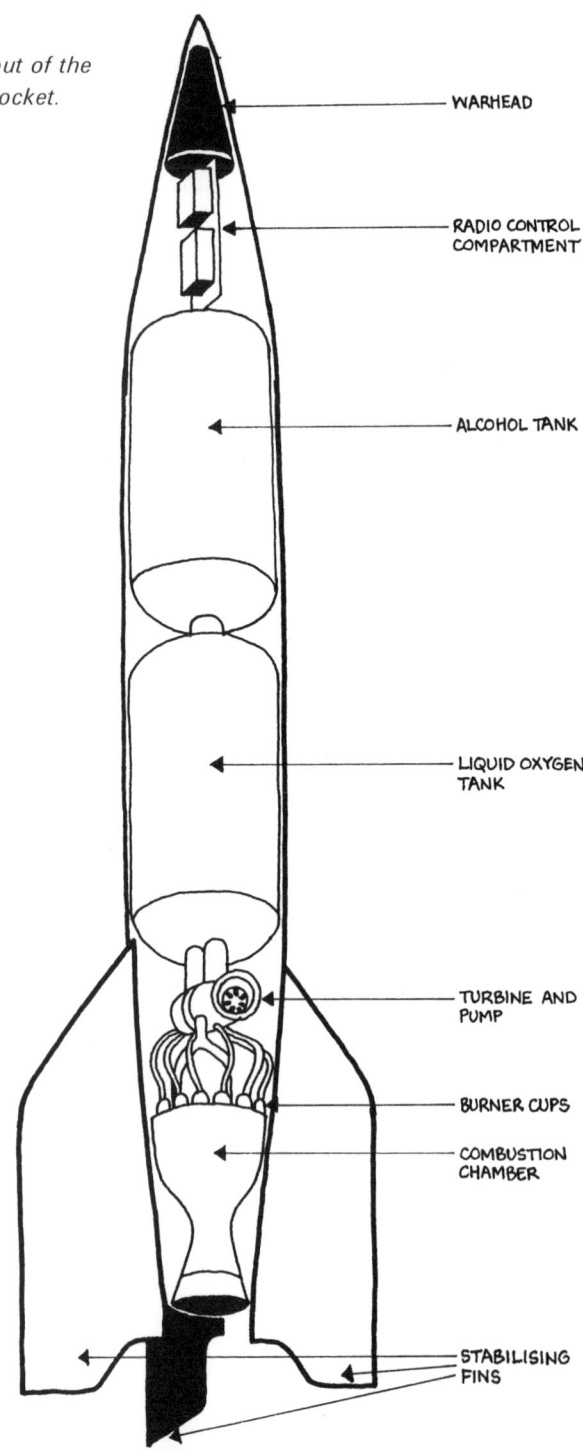

Fig. 38 Layout of the German V2 rocket.

Liquid propellants

Liquid oxygen (Lox) is made by cooling air under pressure till it liquefies. Liquid nitrogen also present will turn back to the gas even more readily than liquid oxygen does (the boiling point of liquid nitrogen, −196 C (77 K), is even lower than that of liquid oxygen, −183 C (90 K). Hence the nitrogen can easily be separated from the oxygen by letting it boil off from the liquid air and then liquefying it again. This is an example of distillation (see Chapter 9). German V2 rockets which bombarded England towards the end of the 1939–45 war used ethyl alcohol as fuel, mixed with water to prevent the combustion chamber getting too hot (see Figure 38).

More modern and powerful rockets use hydrocarbon fuels (compounds of hydrogen and carbon, like petrol or paraffin) or liquid hydrogen. Liquid hydrogen is a more powerful fuel than any hydrocarbon, but is even harder to load and store in the rocket than liquid oxygen since it boils at −253 C (20 K), 70 degrees below the boiling point of liquid oxygen.

Saturn V launch vehicles, which lifted the Apollo astronauts at the start of their journeys to the moon, are three-stage rockets standing 281 feet (86.5 metres) high. The five engines of the first stage burn hydrocarbon fuel and liquid oxygen. During the 160 seconds for which the first stage runs, each engine uses almost three tons of propellants per second. The cluster of five engines gives the first stage a thrust of nearly 3,000 tons at lift-off, increasing to nearly 4,000 tons. After the empty first stage has separated, the second stage continues the journey clear of the earth's atmosphere, in the vacuum of space, almost to earth orbit. Its five engines burn liquid hydrogen and liquid oxygen to give the second stage a thrust of about 500,000 tons, while burning over 400 tons of propellant. The centre engine is fixed but the four clustered around it can be tilted slightly to correct the rocket's course. The main propulsion unit of the third stage is a single engine burning liquid hydrogen and liquid oxygen. It is used twice in a lunar mission; once to place the spacecraft in earth orbit and, again, to move the spacecraft out of earth orbit on course for the moon. The 'brain' of Saturn V is contained in a cylinder 3 feet (approx 1 m) high, nearly 22 feet (7 m) in diameter and weighing nearly 2 tons, on top of the third stage. This contains the guiding, navigating and control equipment to steer the vehicle through its earth orbits and into its final path from earth to the moon.

At lift-off, the Saturn V vehicle weighs about 2,900 tons, of which $\frac{15}{16}$ths are liquid hydrogen and hydrocarbon fuels and liquid oxygen. It is

When speed is vital 85

Apollo—8 lifting off the launch pad at Cape Kennedy in Florida, on a giant Saturn V rocket. (U.S. Information Service Press Office).

capable of carrying a useful load of about 50 tons into lunar orbit—quite a small mass in comparison!

The rocket motors of the Apollo command and lunar modules use compounds of hydrogen and carbon with nitrogen as fuels. These burn spontaneously when mixed with dinitrogen tetroxide (a compound of nitrogen and oxygen which provides the oxygen needed).

Solid propellants

Instead of using volatile liquid fuels and liquid oxygen, rockets can be loaded with solid propellants which contain the oxygen concentrated in the form of one of its solid compounds, mixed with a solid fuel. Or the

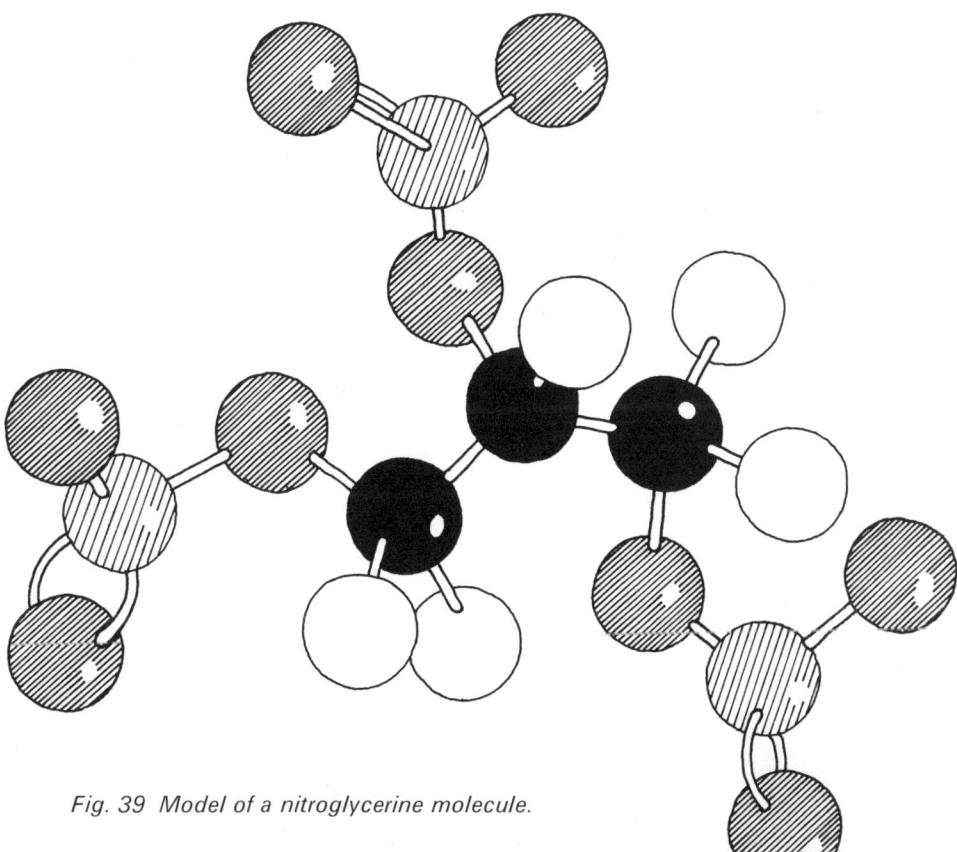

Fig. 39 Model of a nitroglycerine molecule.

oxygen may even be chemically combined with the fuel itself in an unstable way. One such propellant is cordite, a mixture of nitroglycerine and nitrocellulose. The nitroglycerine part consists of molecules made of three carbon atoms, five hydrogen atoms, three nitrogen atoms and nine oxygen atoms, arranged as shown in Figure 39. It is an unstable yellow liquid which is absorbed in the nitrocellulose. Once ignited, it breaks down very quickly to form large volumes of carbon dioxide, steam, nitrogen and spare oxygen and releases a great deal of heat. Figure 40 shows the result of breaking down the model molecule in this way.

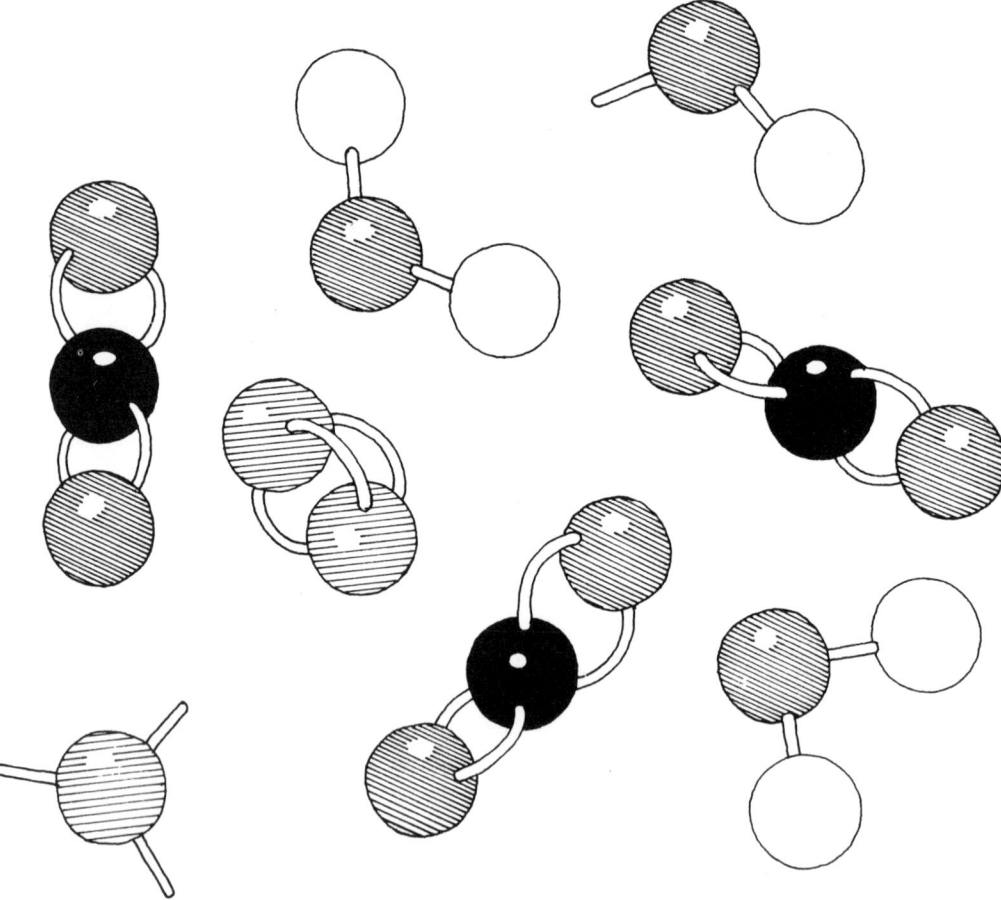

Fig. 40 Models of molecules which can all be obtained from one molecule of nitroglycerine.

Nitrocellulose is a more complicated substance which behaves in a similar way. The result of the sudden change from a solid to a very much larger volume of hot gases blasting from the tail of the rocket is a terrific thrust.

WHAT DO ROCKETS PUSH AGAINST?

Out in space there is hardly any air—so what do the exhaust gases push against when they make the rocket go faster?

Experiment 13: Here is a simple experiment you can try if you have a go-cart. It may help you to answer the question. Collect a set of balls of different masses (e.g. tennis, cricket and soccer) and sit with them on your stationary go-cart on smooth, level ground. Now throw the balls, one at a time, straight in front of you and notice what happens. Try to throw them all with the same speed (one way is to stand a friend about ten metres away and throw to him). Try again, throwing the balls harder (move him back another five metres), and so on.

I expect you found that when you threw a ball in front of you, your go-cart carried you backwards. Because of friction it probably stopped again quite soon. Imagine your go-cart to be a rocket and the ball to be a bit of exhaust gas. Out in space, there is no resistance to your rocket's movement, so it would keep on moving. Each succeeding bit of exhaust gas makes it move faster still. I also hope you found that the harder you threw a ball the faster your go-cart moved and, again, the heavier the ball the faster it moved. With your rocket, the faster the exhaust blast and the greater the mass of gas blown out per second, the better is the acceleration. If you did not have much luck, maybe your go-cart needs oiling?

Now, to return to the question I asked a little while ago. What do rockets push against? You now know what it feels like to throw a ball from a go-cart. When you threw a ball, did you feel that it tried to stay where it was? Because it tended to stay where it was when you threw it forwards, you pushed yourself away from it, backwards. If your rocket had feelings, it would feel a similar sensation when it blew out exhaust gases: the gases would tend to stay where they were and blow the rocket away.

Experiment 14: A Rocket for You to Make. You can make yourself a rocket which squirts out water instead of gases, as follows:

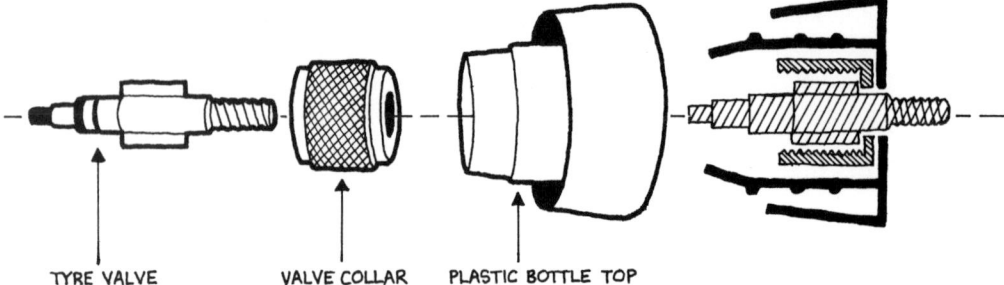

Fig. 41 Fitting the tyre valve into the bottle cap.

For the body of the rocket you need an empty liquid detergent bottle. First of all, fit a bicycle tyre valve to the plastic bottle cap so that you will be able to build up pressure by pumping air into the bottle. To do this, cut off the small nozzle on the cap; put the threaded end of the valve through its valve collar to act as a washer, and push it through the hole in the plastic cap (see Figure 41).

Cut out three fins and a nose cone from thin card, fold and stick them as shown (Figure 42).

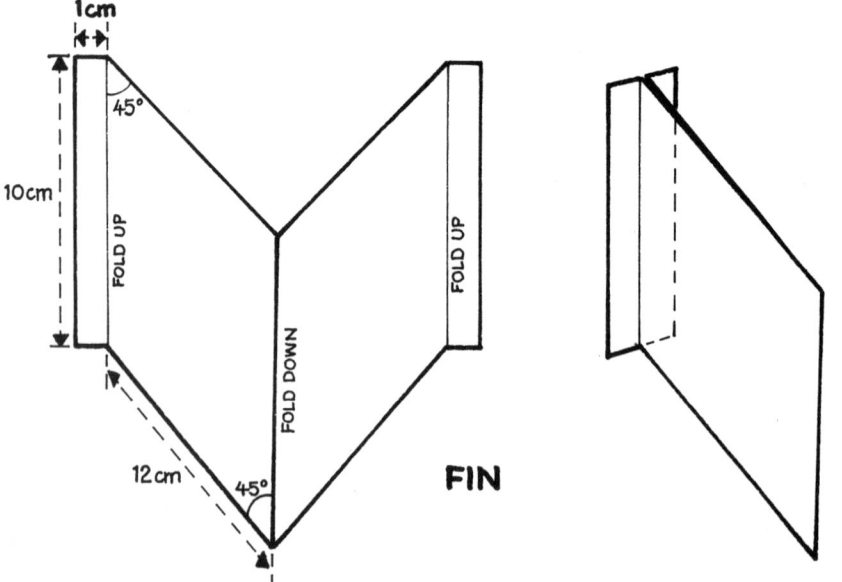

Fig. 42 Details of the construction of a tail fin and the nose cone.

When speed is vital

NOSE CONE

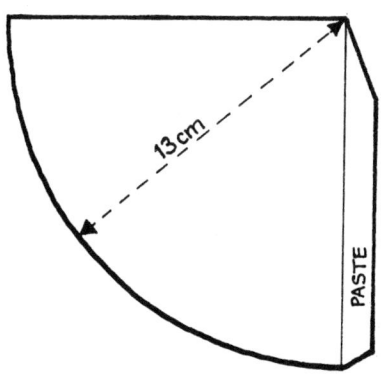
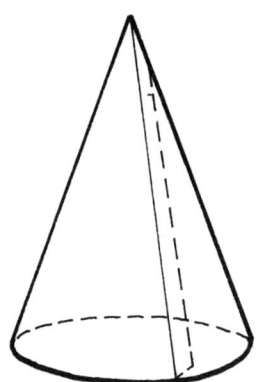

Use 'Copydex' to stick the three fins to the sides of the bottle near the cap, spacing them evenly round the bottle. Stick the nose cone to the base of the bottle. You now have a rocket.

CAUTION: be careful not to let anyone get in the way when you launch your rocket—it takes off fast! Also make sure you have a large clear space in which it can travel without doing damage.

Half fill your rocket with water and push on the plastic cap. Prop up a short plank steeply for a launching ramp and rest the rocket on it. Attach a bicycle pump to the valve and start pumping air into the rocket. When the pressure has built up sufficiently, the cap will blow out and the rocket will shoot up into the air, driven by the force which blows the water out.

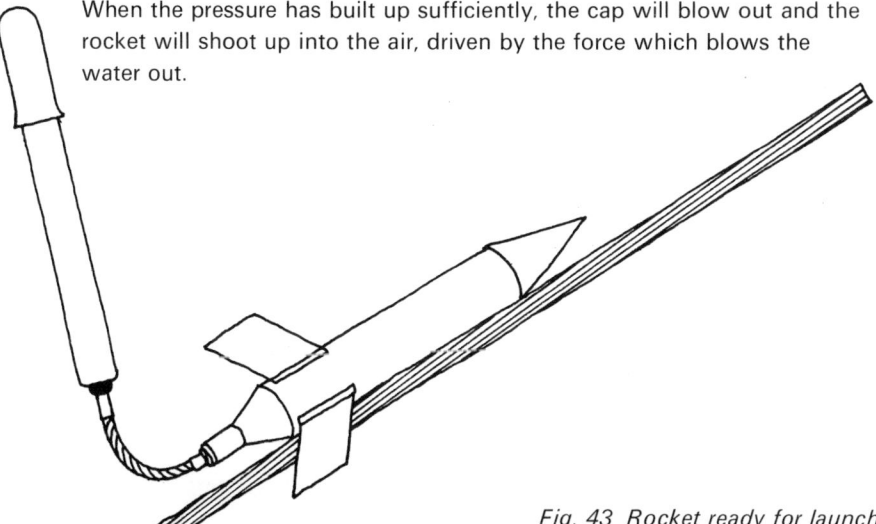

Fig. 43 Rocket ready for launching.

EXPLOSIVES AND EXPLOSIONS

Any of the compounds like nitroglycerine or nitrocellulose, which can break down to give a lot of gases and heat, can be used as an explosive. On the other hand, a mixture of a fuel and some compound which will readily supply it with oxygen will do instead. It only needs sealing in a container together with some means of starting the reaction. HOWEVER, FOR GOODNESS' SAKE DON'T TRY IT! People whose job it is to work with these mixtures know the tricks of handling them, and even they occasionally have unexpected explosions. Some children try making explosives and are lucky in not getting hurt. Others do get hurt or even killed.

A few sticks of cordite, which I mentioned earlier, just flare up momentarily when lit with a match out in the open. Yet cordite sealed up in a cartridge explodes when the firing pin strikes the percussion cap. The expanding hot gases drive the bullet ahead of them up the gun barrel.

Dynamite

If you bump a container of pure nitroglycerine or if it gets hot, it may well explode. This means it is too sensitive an explosive to be handled safely. Dynamite, which is nitroglycerine soaked up in a porous clay, is much more stable and easy to work with and it is widely used in blasting and demolition work.

BOOKS TO READ

You could look up 'Explosive', 'Rocket' and 'Internal Combustion Engine' in an encyclopedia.

Man and Space, Life Science Library (Time-Life International, (Nederland) N.V.)
The section entitled 'The Quickened World of Internal Combustion' in *Machines,* Life Science Library.
The chapter entitled 'The Gas Turbine and its Applications' by D. H. Mallinson in *The Young Scientist,* **3,** edited by W. H. Abbott (Chatto and Windus, London, 1963).
The chapter 'Rocket Propulsion' by H. M. Briscoe in *Young Scientist,* **2** (Chatto and Windus, 1961).
The True Book about Jet Engines and Gas Turbines, Dr E. C. Robinson (Frederick Muller, London).

Ballistic and Guided Missiles, A. Ball, Mechanical Age Library (Frederick Muller, London, 1960).
Rockets and Satellites Work Like This, J. W. R. Taylor (Phoenix House, London).
Jets and Rockets and How They Work, W. F. Gottlieb (John Murray, London).
Rockets and How They Work, Purnell Library of Knowledge (Purnell, 1970).
Man in Space, Henry Brinton (Jarrold and Sons, 1970).
Explosions and Explosives, Brian Morgan, Quantum Books, **8** (Macmillan, 1967).
The Modern World, *Jets,* Charles S. Verrall (Frederick Muller, 1966).
Rockets and Missiles, John W. R. Taylor, Hamlyn All-Colour Paperbacks (Hamlyn, 1970).
How it Works, the Rocket, David Carey, Ladybird Books (Wills & Hepworth, 1967).

8 COAL

HOW COAL WAS FORMED

There used to be a large, warm, sunny swamp where Lancashire and Yorkshire are today. Things have changed a lot since then—but they have had about two hundred and fifty million years in which to do it. Lush vegetation grew quickly. There were forests of giant club mosses, tree-ferns and horsetails (other plants with fern-like leaves, but which bore seeds) and the ancestors of our fir trees.

As the plants flourished and died, and others took their places, so their remains collected under the water in which they had stood during their lives. As they decayed bubbles of carbon dioxide, methane and hydrogen rose to the surface. Under the stagnant water they could not rot away completely because hardly any oxygen reached them from the air. As the

Fig. 44 Diagram of the structure of the Pennine coalfield.

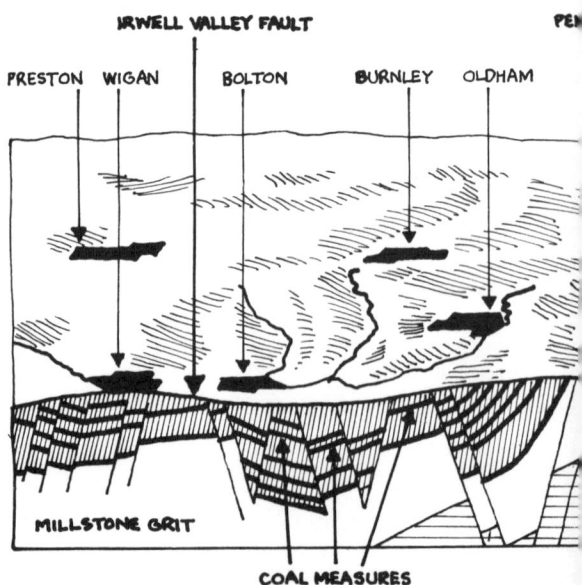

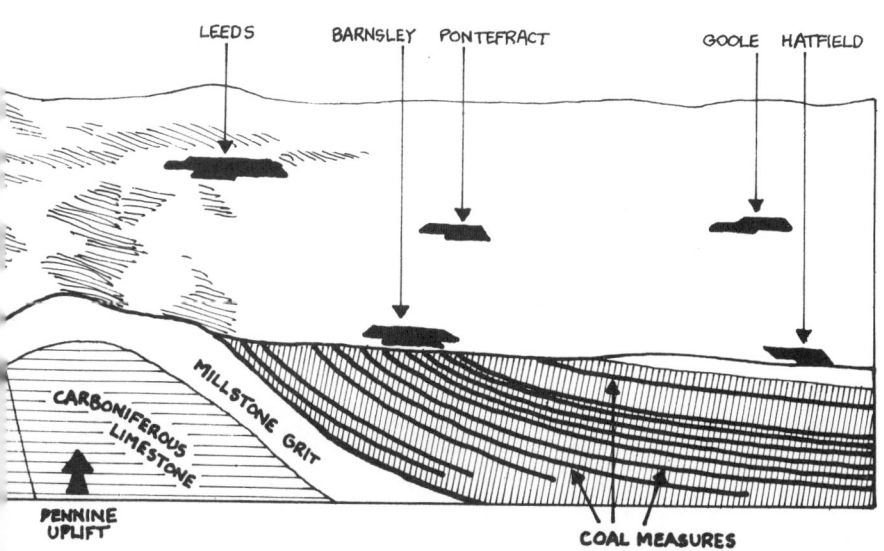

Impression of a coal-forming forest. (Courtesy of the National Coal Board)

Fern-like fossils found in coal measures. Courtesy of the National Coal Board)

layer of plant debris grew thicker, so the earth's crust sank under its weight. The lower parts of the layer changed slowly to brown or black peat, under the pressure from ever more material collecting on the top.

Occasionally the swamps became flooded too deeply for the forest to survive: perhaps the land subsided too quickly? Anyway the layer of peat became covered by a layer of mud and gravel. Later, the water subsided, forests established themselves again, and a fresh layer of peat began to form. This happened again and again, so that layer after layer of peat became covered by mud or sand. As fresh layers buried old, so the pressure on

Coal

the older, lower layers increased at a rate of about 144 lb per square inch (10 Bar) for each increase in depth of 117 feet (35.7 m). The temperature of the layers increased as they became buried deeper, too: rising by about 1 °C for every 117 feet increase in depth. As the pressure on the peat increased and it grew warmer, water and other volatile compounds were driven out so that the peat slowly became harder, blacker and richer in carbon: in other words, it was turned into coal.

The earth's crust is not a good fit: as the middle of the earth cools and shrinks, the crust is forced to wrinkle from time to time. One big wrinkle forced its way up through the layers I have just been talking about, and formed the Pennine range of hills and mountains which divides Yorkshire from Lancashire.

As you can see in Figure 44, on the Yorkshire side of the Pennines the coalfield is in a fairly undamaged state but on the Lancashire side it has lots of cracks (or 'faults'): large chunks of the coalfield have moved up or down by thousands of feet.

Other large coal-producing areas in Britain are in Scotland, Northumberland and Durham, Staffordshire and the South Midlands, and South Wales. These provide a complete range of 'ranks' of coal from low ranking brown coal, which is rather like peat, to high ranking anthracite, in which few traces of original plants can be found.

HOW COAL REPLACED CHARCOAL AS A FUEL

The original fuel used to smelt metals from their ores was charcoal. This is the solid you are left with if you heat carbon-containing animal or vegetable matter, while keeping the air out. It is essentially an impure form of carbon. Charcoal burners were men who worked in the woods and forests. They stacked up heaps of wood, partly covering them with earth to limit the amount of air getting in. Then they set fire to the heaps. The heat produced as part of the wood burned turned the rest to charcoal.

We cannot be sure when coal was first recognised as a fuel, but it has certainly been in use for a long time. Coalfields were being worked in England, Scotland and the mainland of Europe at the beginning of the thirteenth century. Ashes of coal fires have been found in Roman remains excavated in England. The ancient Greek smiths sometimes used a 'black stone' from Greece and Northern Italy instead of charcoal, and the Chinese are said to have used coal in 1,000 BC.

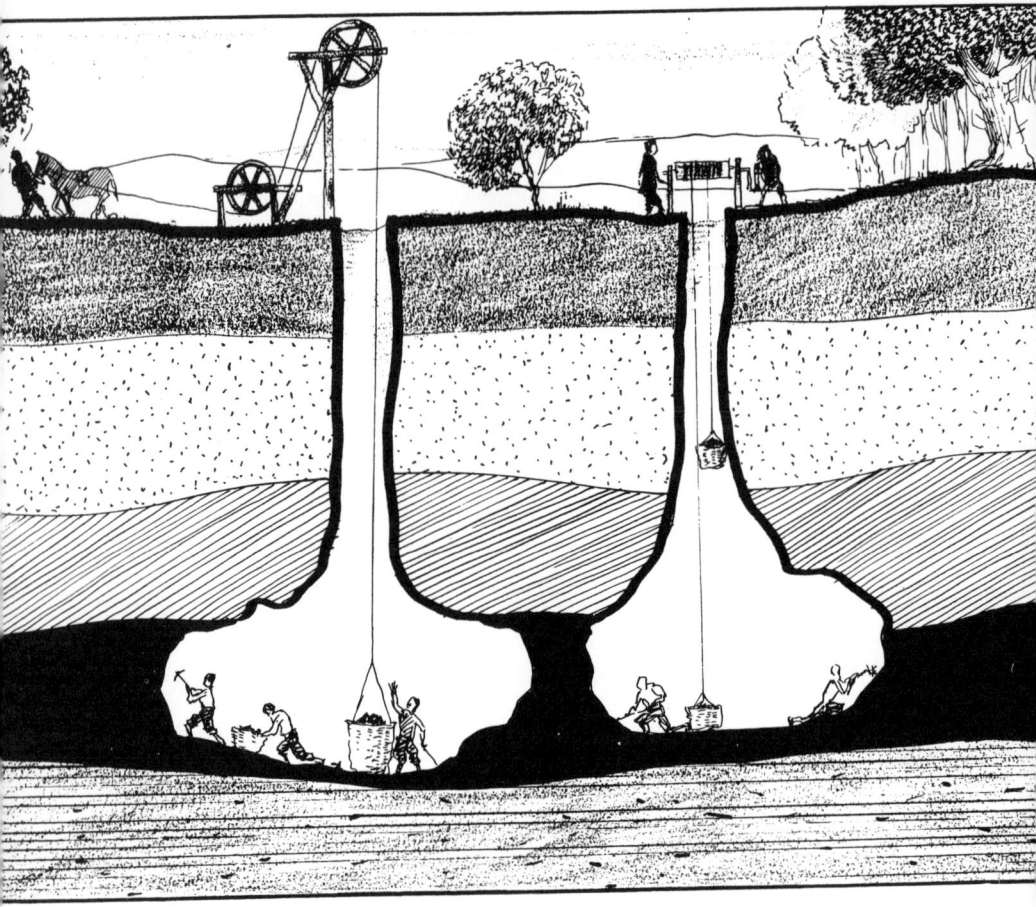

Fig. 45 Impression of bell pits (Courtesy of the National Coal Board)

Men would first have taken coal from exposed seams, in cliffs on the coast for example. They could not take much without the cliff they were undermining falling on them. Later, men dug down through the ground where they thought a coal seam was near the surface. When they reached the coal they dug it out and hauled it to the surface in baskets.
Thus the hole became wider at the base, something like a bell shape (Figure 45).

At first, people did not have chimneys to remove the unpleasant fumes and smoke which coal fires emit. This made coal unpopular and most people burned wood instead. During the reign of Edward I (1239–1307) you would have been hanged if you had been caught burning coal.

Coal

During the reign of the Tudors (fifteenth and sixteenth centuries) coal became needed more and more for firing brick kilns. When these bricks were used to build fireplaces and chimneys, domestic coal fires became popular so the demand for coal increased still further.

DANGER AND DISCOMFORT DOWN THE MINE

In the early days of mining, miners worked according to whatever rules seemed fit to the owner of the land underneath which the coal lay.
It was hard, uncomfortable and very dangerous work, cutting coal in poorly lit, badly ventilated, narrow underground galleries. Apart from the risk of being crushed if the roof fell in, or drowned if the mine was flooded, there were the risks of being suffocated in 'blackdamp' or being blown up in a 'firedamp' explosion.

Blackdamp is a mixture of carbon dioxide and nitrogen, containing no oxygen, which tends to collect in mines unless it is pumped out.

Explosion of Fire Damp ('Underground Life or Mines and Miners' by L. Simonin)

Firedamp is methane gas formed as the vegetation turned to coal and released when the coal is cut. A naked light brought into air containing 5 to 15 per cent of methane will cause an explosion. A small explosion of firedamp could then ignite a much more violent explosion of the ever-present coal dust in the air and so spread disaster through the mine. If he survived all these dangers, a miner would still, very likely, develop a lung disease because of the dust he had breathed regularly during his working days.

As the demand for coal grew, so pits were sunk deeper. As a result, the water seeping in had to be pumped out continuously to prevent flooding. The miners' chances of being killed or injured became still greater. In the eighteenth century pumps invented for the purpose began to be worked by steam engines. Because these engines proved so useful in other ways, the Industrial Revolution began producing an even bigger demand for coal.

THE INDUSTRIAL REVOLUTION

Coke was needed to smelt the iron from which machinery was made and the iron bridges which spanned rivers. Large factories powered by coal-fired steam engines sprang up. Steel rails stretched out across Britain, enabling coal-fired trains to carry raw materials and finished goods where they were needed, and bringing people closer together. Larger and larger coal-fired iron ships improved trade steadily with the rest of the world. As the Industrial Revolution grew so did the need for coal.

MINING DURING THE INDUSTRIAL REVOLUTION

Child Labour

Can you remember how you spent your ninth birthday? Whether term-time or holiday, I expect you spent a part of the day out of doors in fresh air and daylight—and perhaps you had a party?

If you had been living in a mining village at the beginning of the nineteenth century, your ninth birthday would have been spent, like most of the previous years, working in a coal mine for as much as twelve hours of the day: your parents would have been so poor that you would have had to go down to start earning as soon as possible; and that would be your future, too. It was the custom in those days for children of eight to work down the mine, and quite common for them to start even as early as

Tapping molten iron from a blast furnace. (Courtesy of the National Coal Board)

seven. Women worked there, too. You would have begun your working life as a trapdoor keeper—whose job was to stay in the dark by one of the trapdoors which controlled the ventilation and open it whenever someone wanted to pull a truck through. Later on you would have been put to 'hurrying'—dragging trucks, perhaps on all fours, along a roadway only 30 inches (80 cm) high.

Robert Drury was $10\frac{1}{2}$ years old in 1841. This is how he described his life in the Yorkshire coalfield: 'I trap in the pit. I don't like it because it's in the dark, it isn't hard work; I do nothing else but trap. I go sometimes at six in the morning; on Saturdays I go at five, and I come out after six in the evening, sometimes before. They use me well in the pit, they never beat me. I've bread and cheese, or treacle, or potatoes and meat, when I can get it, for dinner; I go to a Sunday school and used to go to a day school before I went to the pit. Jesus Christ was God. He came to earth lately. Heaven is Jesus Christ; I shall go there when I die if I'm a good boy and to hell if I'm bad. I don't know what this country is called, nor what is the chief town.'

Ventilation

Nowadays, mines are well ventilated. They always have two shafts ('downcast' and 'upcast'). Big fans in the upcast shaft suck used air and dangerous gases out of the mine and discharge them at the surface. So fresh air goes down the downcast shaft and sweeps through all the galleries. Most collieries used to have a furnace burning in the upcast shaft. This heated air which rose up the shaft, carrying other gases with it, while fresh air entered the mine down the downcast shaft. Miners going up or down the shaft found the heat, smoke and gases extremely unpleasant, and the ropes tended to get damaged, too, so the best collieries used a special shaft, called the 'drawing' shaft, for the furnace, instead.

To prevent the fresh air making short cuts to the furnace and leaving part of the mine unventilated, trapdoors had to be fitted in some of the galleries so that the draught tended to blow them shut. However, even in a well-regulated pit, miners were known to prop trapdoors open to prevent a good ventilating draught at the coal face because it made their candles run; the temperature at the coal face was over 70 F (21 C).

Lighting

Miners working by candlelight ran the risk of firedamp explosions. Firedamp (methane gas) is less dense than air so it tended to hang about just under the roof of the gallery. Here it could be burned (with luck)

The 'penitent' igniting firedamp. (from 'Underground Life' by Simonin)

because it was probably not mixed with enough air to cause an explosion. One dangerous way of clearing a gallery of firedamp was for a miner (called the 'penitent') to crawl through, his clothes soaked in water, holding up near the roof a lighted candle tied to a stick.

A safe way of illuminating mines was invented by Sir Humphry Davy, about 1815 to 1816. He fitted a metal gauze around the flame from an oil lamp. Air needed to keep the flame alight could get in through the gauze. The gauze conducted the heat of the flame away so that it could not ignite any methane mixed with the air outside the gauze. However, the safety afforded was thrown away by miners who poked holes in both sides of the gauze of their safety lamps so that they could blow the flame through and light their pipes.

THE FIGHT TO IMPROVE WORKING CONDITIONS

The awful conditions affected miners so that the rest of society looked on them as outcasts. However, suffering tends to draw a group of people closer together. From time to time, groups of miners tried to improve their working conditions by striking or by sending a petition to the king—but with no real success.

The first big step forward was when the miners spread the Methodist Church's gospel of salvation in their villages. Because of it, a great many miners improved the sort of lives they lived. It was largely from these men that the early Trade Unions drew their leadership.

The second step was the setting up of a Royal Commission in 1840, to report to Parliament on the employment of women and children underground.

The third was the formation, by Martin Jude in 1841, of the Miners' Association of Great Britain. From it stem the characteristic policies of trying to improve conditions through Acts of Parliament rather than through strikes; and of insisting on continuous negotiation with employers.

One of the greatest 19th-century fighters for better living and working conditions for ordinary people was Anthony Ashley Cooper, 7th Earl of Shaftesbury. When the Royal Commission made its report in 1842 on mining conditions, the public was shocked by what it revealed. Through the Earl of Shaftesbury's iniative the Mines Act was passed preventing the employment underground of females of all ages and of boys under ten years old. The Act also provided for mines inspectors to be appointed.

COAL MINING IN BRITAIN TODAY

Most of the high quality coal seams which can be got at easily in this country have now been exhausted. We have even been drilling the seabed to try to find workable seams which could be mined by tunnelling out to them from the shore.

Conditions in coal mines are much easier and far safer today. Machines are used which cut the coal from the coalface and load it onto conveyors in one operation; the pick and shovel belong in the museum. A plough, ot trepanner, or shearer moves along the coalface, its teeth cutting off a slice of coal the thickness of the seam. It throws the coal on to a conveyor running beside it along the coalface. This conveyor unloads it on to another one which carries the coal to the trucks and loads them. The roof at the coalface is supported by props like big hydraulic jacks. As the cutting machine passes by, every second prop is moved forward by a big hydraulic ram, to support the new part of the roof. Then the conveyor is pushed forward and the rest of the props are moved up, too.

The cutting machine has teeth at both ends, so it is ready to return, making a fresh cut. In some collieries these machines and the props are worked by remote control, so coal can be produced with no one present at the coalface.

Trepanner working at the coalface. The hydraulic props which hold up the roof can also be clearly seen. (Courtesy of the National Coal Board)

Instead of being pushed along in small tubs carrying only a few
hundredweight, coal is now hauled underground by locomotives, in mine
cars which can carry from 30 cwt to 6 tons.

If possible, the unsupported roof behind the props is allowed to fall in.
However, most of our coalfields lie under industrial areas—because the coal
is right there to be used. The trouble is that when coal is taken out,
the ground tends to subside into the space left, which would damage and
disrupt the buildings and businesses on the surface. Machines are used to
pack rubble tightly into the spaces behind the props: this reduces surface
subsidence a lot but cannot stop it completely.

HOW IS THE COAL USED?

Most of the coal brought out of the mine goes straight to power stations
where it is burned to provide steam for the turbines which drive the
electricity generators. The rest of the coal has to be cleaned of the pieces
of metal which become fixed with it, by passing it under an electromagnet.
Then it is washed and sorted to remove dirt and rocks. Finally it is
separated into various size grades ranging from lumps down to dust. A lot
goes to coke ovens which produce the coke needed to smelt iron in blast
furnaces. Less and less is being used in gas works, because the supply of
natural gas is increasing. The rest is used as fuel for steam engines and
for heating homes, offices and factories.

PLACES TO VISIT

If you ever get a chance to go down a coal mine, do not miss it.
However, this sort of trip is more easily arranged for a school party than
for an individual.

The Science Museum, South Kensington, London, SW7 2DD, has a section
on mining, on the lower ground floor, also a fine collection of coal-fired
steam engines (pumps used for draining mines, and railway engines).

BOOKS TO READ

The National Coal Board Public Relations Department, Hobart House,
Grosvenor Place, London, S.W.1, supplies an interesting range of booklets,
films and wall charts, preferably to schools rather than individuals, including
one booklet full of suggestions for a project on 'coal'.

Look through 'Jackdaw' No. 7, *Shaftesbury and the Working Children*, compiled and edited by John Langdon-Davies (Jonathan Cape, 30, Bedford Square, London, W.C.1.)

Look up 'Coal' in an encyclopedia.

Nuffield Foundation's Chemistry Background Books, *Coal*, H. Donaldson and H. B. Locke; and *Humphrey Davy* (Longmans/Penguin Books, London).
The Industrial Revolution, 1760–1860, M. E. Beggs Humphreys (George Allen and Unwin, Ltd., London).
Behind the Scenes in a Coalmine, J. Newell (Phoenix House, London).
Reference Geographies, *Mining for Coal in Britain,* R. S. Goodwin (Chatto and Windus, London, 1964).
Coal, E. F. Carter, Mechanical Age Library (Frederick Muller Ltd., London, 1963).
Minerals, Mines and Mining, Approaches to Environmental Studies, Book II, G. A. Perry (Blandford Press, 1971).
Coal Mining, John Davey (A & C Black, 1966).
Coal Mines and Miners, Miles Tomalin, Methuen's Outlines (Methuen, 1966).
The Industrial Revolution, Peter Lane, Visual Sources Series (Batsford, 1972).

9 OIL

Fig. 46 Oil traps
1. Oil trapped underneath a dome of impermeable rock.
2. A 'fault trap' occurs when a break in the strata brings an impermeable sealing layer opposite a sloping porous layer.
3. A layer of impermeable rock has sealed the end of a layer of porous rock and trapped oil in it.
4. A plug of salt under pressure has pushed up through the layers of rock. Oil collects in the sloping porous layers, where they have been sealed by the salt plug.

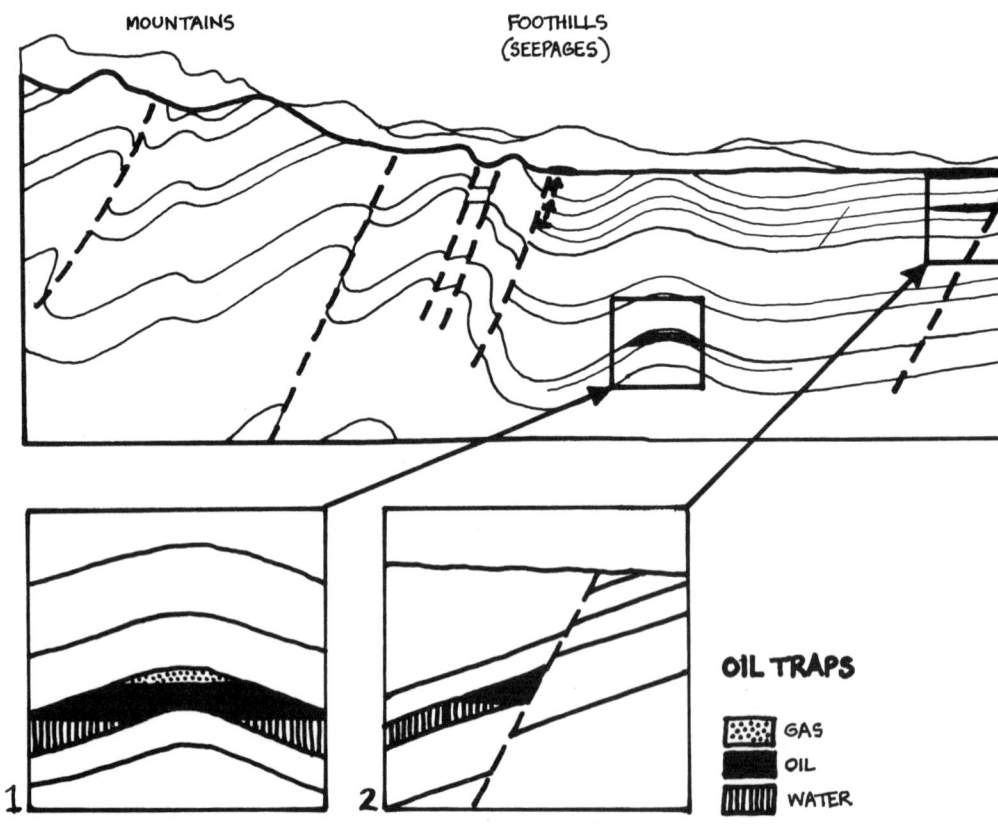

Oil

WHAT IS OIL?

Crude oil is found in layers of rock below ground. This is why it is called 'petroleum': the name is made up from the Latin words petra (rock) and oleum (oil). Most of the world's oil has been formed during the past 200 million years.

Not much is found in rocks older than this and none in rocks more than 500 million years old.

It is a mixture of a great many volatile substances, mainly hydrocarbons. A hydrocarbon is a compound made entirely of carbon and hydrogen, and nothing else. Here and there petroleum seeps through the rocks to the surface. For instance, at Baku in Russia, and Kirkuk in Iraq the ground is alight with flames fed by petroleum gas continually escaping from below.

FORELAND (ACCUMULATIONS)

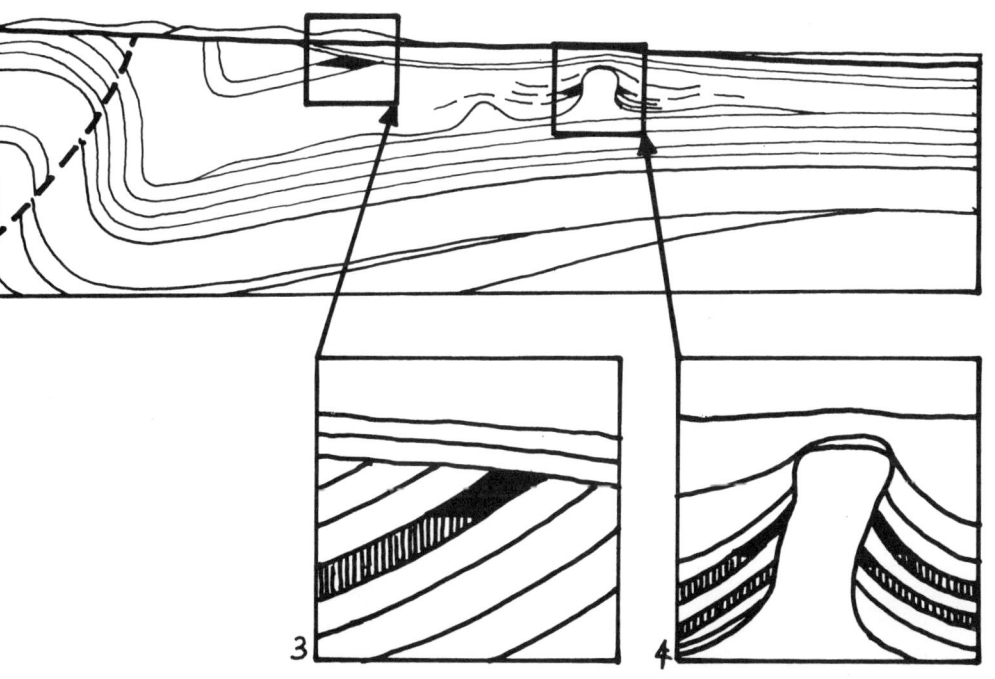

These fires, possibly first lit by flashes of lightning, have been burning for centuries and will burn for many more. Lake Asphalt in Trinidad is all that is left of an ancient petroleum seepage. The more volatile part evaporated long ago leaving a vast, sticky lake of pitch.

HOW WAS PETROLEUM FORMED?

The sea is full of microscopic plants and animals, continually multiplying and dying. Petroleum comes from the countless millions of them who died, sank to the sea bed and became silted over with clay. The silt kept the oxygen out as their soft bodies decayed. As the layers of sediment piled up above them, the pressure on their remains grew and the temperature rose. The clay was slowly turned to shale, and oil was squeezed out of the decayed organisms.

Porous rocks like sandstone are full of very small holes and channels, which contain water. Since oil floats on water, the squeezed-out oil rises up through the water in the layers of porous rock above it. Eventually it reaches the surface—unless it comes up against a layer of impermeable rock, rock through which water cannot pass. Then it seeps sideways until either it finds a way of escape, or it becomes trapped. Figure 46 shows some typical oil traps.

HOW IS OIL FOUND?

There is no way of knowing for sure whether there is oil under a particular piece of ground without actually drilling. Otherwise, the best one can do is to decide whether the rock formations are promising or not and to detect any folds or faults which could trap any oil that might be there. To drill an exploratory hole in out-of-the-way country could cost £100 a foot (£330 a metre), so a 10,000 ft (3,000 metre) deep hole would cost £1 million. Obviously you must be careful to drill only in sensible spots!

Sometimes, as in Iran, oil-bearing strata are close to the surface and fairly easy to study. More often, they are so deeply buried that what you see on the surface tells you very little about where to drill.

The pull of gravity varies slightly, from place to place, depending on the density of the rocks making up the earth's crust. One way of finding out the distribution of underground rocks is to measure very slight changes in the force of gravity at different points on the surface.

Measuring changes in the strength and direction of the earth's magnetic field using a sensitive airborne magnetometer. (British Petroleum Co. photograph)

Another way of surveying the distribution of rocks is to map local variations in the strength and direction of the earth's magnetic field. This depends on the local disturbances which magnetic iron ores make in this field.

A very important method is seismic surveying. Charges are exploded in the ground. The shock waves spread downwards and outwards and are reflected or echoed up again by every surface between rock layers. Special microphones, called geophones, strung out in a line on the surface record all these echoes. From the results it is possible to work out the depths of the various layers.

DRILLING FOR OIL

In the end, you must drill in the most likely places before you can know whether oil is there or not. The drill is a long pipe with a cutting tool, called a 'bit', at the end (Figure 47). The bit bites its

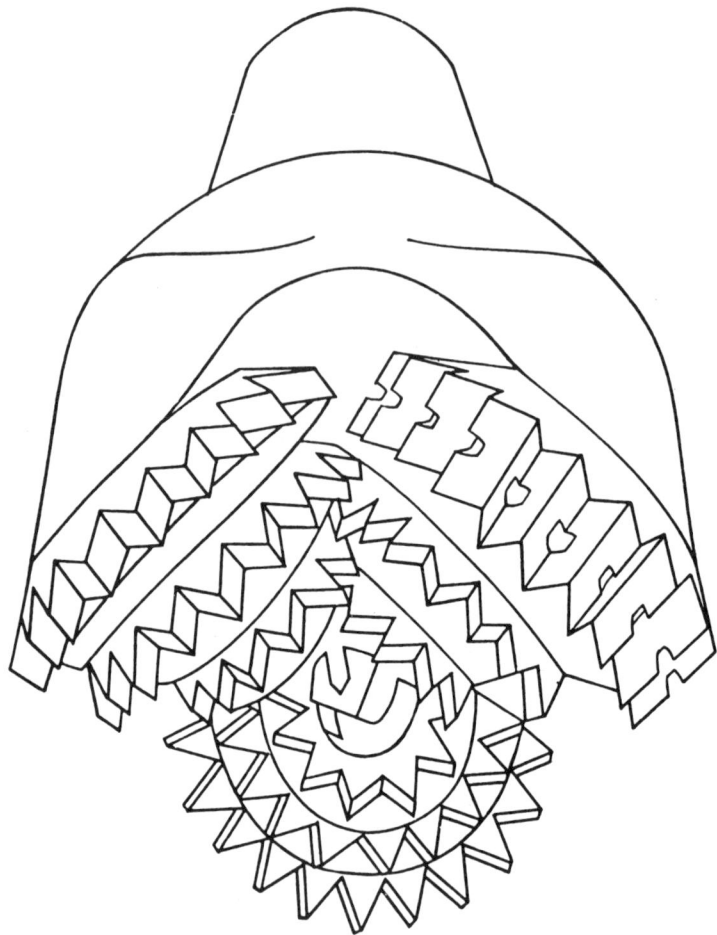

Fig. 47 Diagram of a drilling bit (Courtesy of British Petroleum Co.)

way down into the ground when the pipe is turned by an engine at the surface. A continuous stream of mud pumped down the pipe flows round the bit, cools and lubricates it (Figure 48). Then the mud squirts up the hole outside the pipe, bringing out pieces of rock broken off by the bit. The mud also helps prevent the sides of the well collapsing and prevents oil or gas blowing out of the drill cuts through to rock containing them under pressure. Above the drill is a derrick which handles the extra lengths of pipe needed as the drill bites deeper. Apart from the waste and risk of fire, a blow-out could easily destroy the derrick.

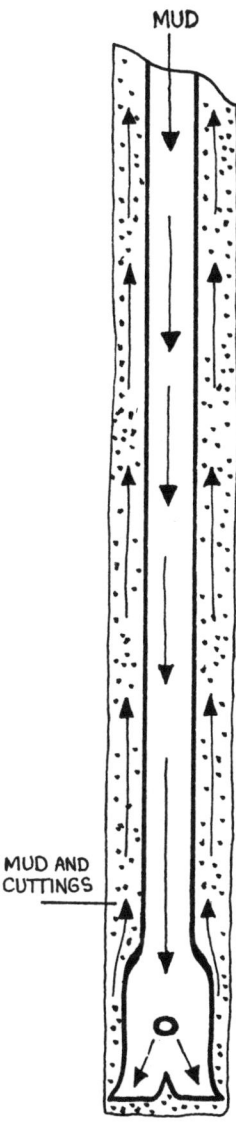

Fig. 48 Mud circulating round a drill bit and removing cuttings from the hole.

Blow-out at Naft Safid oil well. The tangled line in the air is the drill pipe blown out of the ground by the pressure. (British Petroleum Co. photograph)

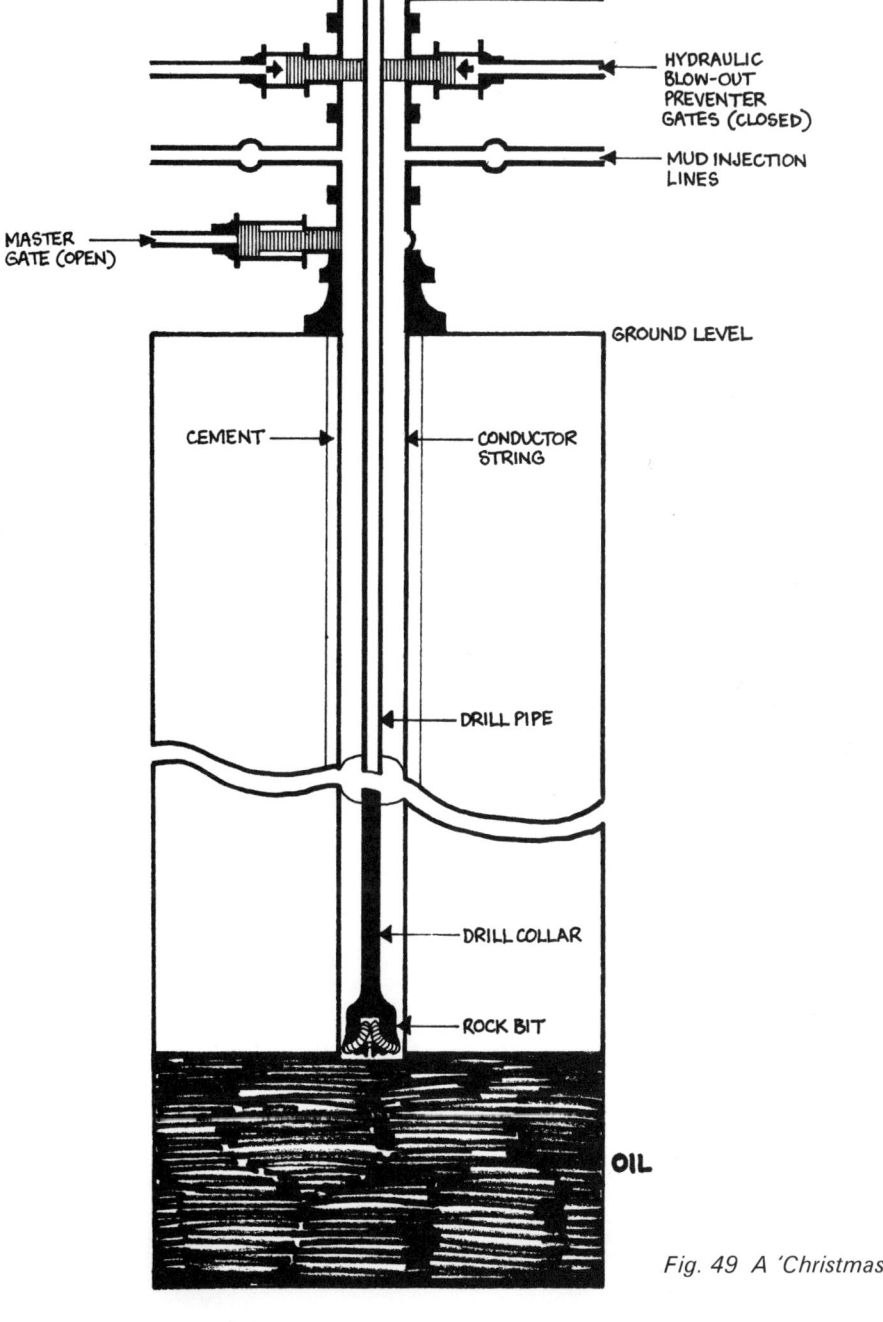

Fig. 49 A 'Christmas tree'.

After drilling a short distance down, a steel conductor pipe (conductor string) about 16 inches (40 cm) in diameter is lowered into the well. Cement slurry is pumped into the space between it and the wall of the well to lock the pipe in place. When the cement has set, a 'Christmas tree' is fixed to the top of the conductor pipe. It gets its name from the pipes sticking out all round it rather like the branches of a fir tree. These include pipes through which the mud is pumped in and allowed out, and pipes to work a hydraulic blow-out preventer to seal the well if there is a blow-out while drilling (Figure 49). In a deep well two or more steel lining pipes may be needed to protect the walls as the bit digs down further. If oil is found, a perforator screen pipe is lowered right into the hole in the oil-bearing sand. This allows oil and gas in but keeps the sand out. Lastly, a pipe about 2 inches (5 cm) in diameter is run all the way down to the screen pipe and water is pumped down to wash out the mud.

If the pressure is high, oil now starts to flow naturally. As the oil is taken away, so the pressure in the underground oil trap falls. Eventually the pressure becomes too low and the oil has to be pumped out in some way. Figure 50 shows several ways in which this is done. In the 'gas-lift' method, gas is pumped down between the inner tube and the casing: it mixes with the oil and brings it to the surface. Alternatively, a lift pump may be used. In the 'injection' methods the oil pressure is increased again either by pumping gas down to press down on the surface of the oil, or by pumping water down to push it up from underneath.

Fig. 50 Different ways in which oil is brought out of the ground.

Oil

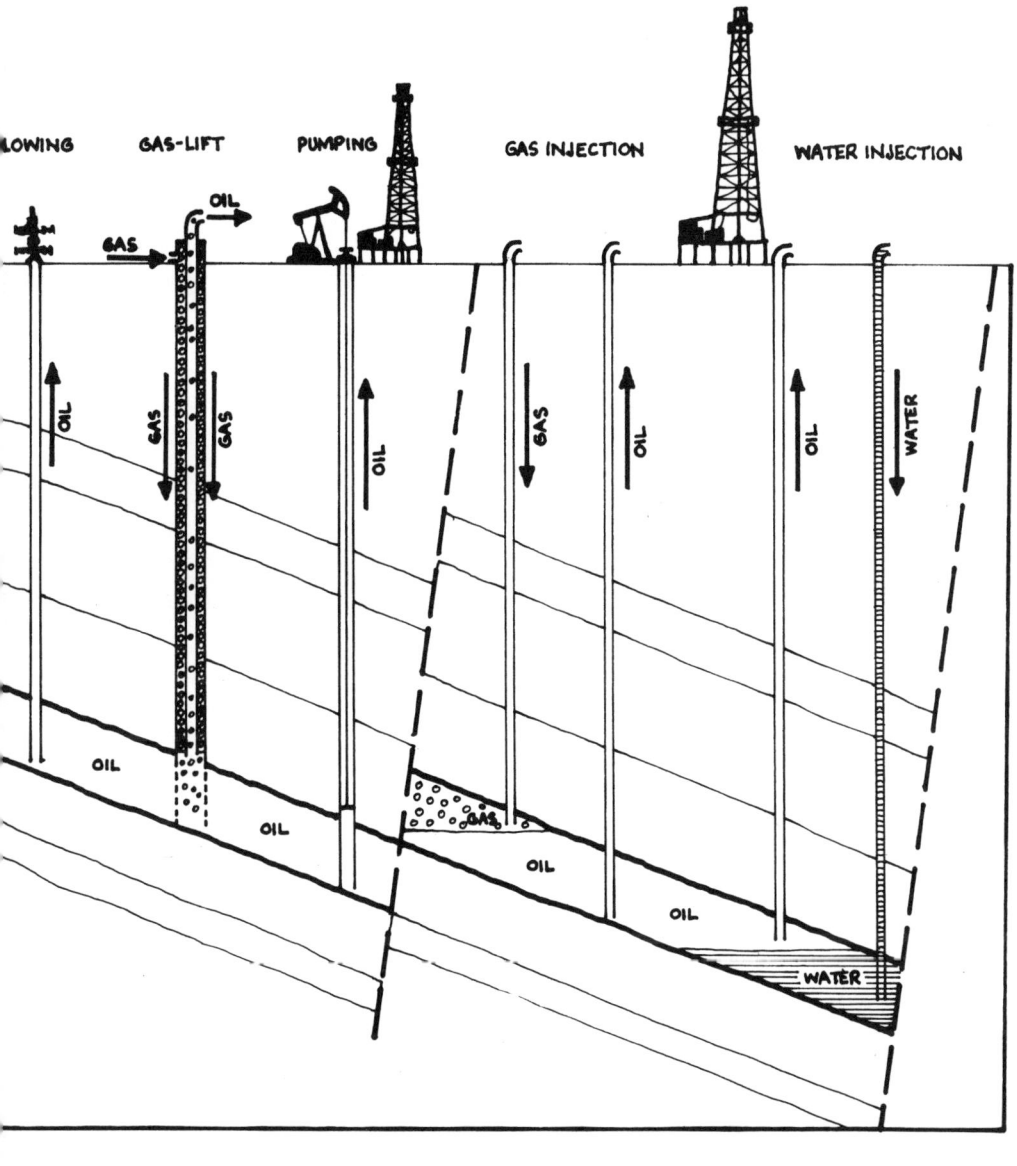

Fire and Fuels

TRANSPORTING CRUDE OIL

Crude oil must be taken to refineries and then the refined products must be taken to the consumers. Some oil refineries are built beside oil fields but most are built beside the industrial centres which need the oil. These centres are generally thousands of miles from any rich oil field so the crude oil is piped overland to the nearest port and then shipped in large tankers. Nearly one third of the world's merchant shipping is made up of tankers.

Oil

BP Tanker Company's 100,000 ton BRITISH ARGOSY arriving at Angle Bay Ocean Terminal, Pembrokeshire. (British Petroleum Co. photograph)

Catalytic Cracker Unit at BP's Kent Oil Refinery. (British Petroleum Co. photograph)

Oil

REFINING CRUDE OIL

Distillation

We first met this method of separating mixed liquids in Chapter 7—there it was used to separate oxygen from liquid air. At the refinery crude oil is distilled to separate it into different fractions, each one having its own short range of boiling point. To do this, crude oil is vaporised by a furnace and the vapour is passed into a tall tower full of trays with holes in. Each hole is covered by a 'bubble cap'. The column is hottest at the bottom, gradually becoming cooler further up and is coolest at the top. When the vapour comes in, it passes through the bubble caps and begins to spread through the column. The tower cools it down as it goes up so some of the substances in the vapour begin to liquefy because the temperature in that part of the tower is below their boiling

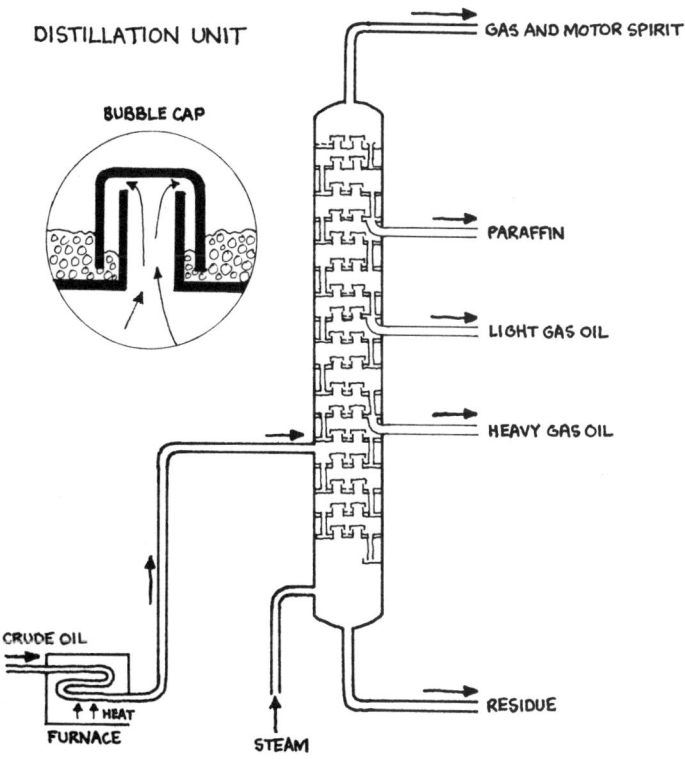

Fig. 51 Diagram of a typical distallation unit.

points. Further up, the column is cooler still so more substances are forced to liquefy. Only the most volatile ones can reach the top. The bubble caps make sure nothing can get higher up the column than its boiling point entitles it. In this way, all the substances in crude oil are spread out up the column from the least volatile at the bottom to the most volatile at the top. Crude oil vapour is passed in continuously. At certain points up the side of the tower, gas oil, paraffin and naphtha fractions are run off continuously; fuel oil is run out at the bottom and motor spirit is taken off at the top. Figure 51 shows diagrammatically how a typical distillation unit works.

Cracking

Motor spirit (petrol) is mainly made up of hydrocarbons with eight carbon atoms and eighteen hydrogen atoms in their molecules. We need more of it than crude oil provides naturally.

In refineries, some of the hydrocarbons containing larger molecules are 'cracked' (broken) to give us the smaller molecules we want. Details vary, but generally the heavier hydrocarbon vapour is heated with a catalyst in a plant called a catalytic cracker. The catalyst helps the hydrocarbon molecules to break up more easily, at a lower temperature than they could without it. Catalytic crackers are designed to run continuously: the more volatile liquids and gases are led off as they are formed to make room for more of the heavy oil.

Other catalytic plants rearrange atoms within the molecules to make them into more efficient fuels. Simple zig-zag chains are changed into branched ones or their ends are joined to make rings.

The products

Finally, any traces of harmful substances have to be removed before the products are sold. For example, sulphur compounds must be removed from fuels because they form poisonous, acidic sulphur dioxide when they are burned.

The main fuels obtained from petroleum are: petroleum gases, e.g. Calor gas, Gaz; motor spirit (petrol); paraffin; gas oil, used as diesel fuel and supplied to the gas industry to be turned into gas; and fuel oil, used to heat boilers.

Apart from these, lubricating oils, waxes for polishes and candles, and bitumen are important products.

Oil

THINGS TO DO

If you live within reach of an oil refinery, you could try to arrange a visit for your school or club.

You could write to the Public Relations Departments of the major oil companies in this country, to see if they would supply you with instructive booklets or wall charts. Some companies will lend films to schools.

BOOKS TO READ

Look up Petroleum in an encyclopedia.

Read the chapter called 'The Story of Oil' by Dr L. V. W. Clark, in *The Young Scientist,* **2.** Then read the chapter called 'Chemicals From Petroleum' by Dr L. L. Katan, in *The Young Scientist,* **3.** Edited by W. Abbott, Chatto and Windus, London, 1963.
The Nuffield Chemistry Background Book, *Petroleum,* H. P. H. Oliver (Longmans/Penguin Books, London).
Oil From The Ground, H. Adams (Basil Blackwell, Oxford, 1962).
How We Get and Use Oil, D. Le Roi (Routledge and Kegan Paul, 1962).
It's Made Like This: 'Petrol and Oils', G. Walmsley (John Baker, London, 1967).
Oil, Henry Kurth, Children's University (Windmill Press, 1972).
How They Were Built, Wells, Chapter 4, 5 and 6, John Stuart Murphy and Charles Keeping (O.U.P., 1965).

10 GAS

WHAT IS 'GAS'?

At one time, nearly all this country's gas came from coal—so it was called 'coal gas'. Now, less than half of it comes from coal and the proportion is decreasing still further—so we will call it 'town gas' instead.

WHERE DOES TOWN GAS COME FROM?

There are three main methods of producing town gas:
(i) heating coal strongly to break it up into coke, gas and other products (carbonising);
(ii) turning coal or oil completely into gas (gasification); and
(iii) tapping natural gas.

(i) Carbonising coal

In this method, which is becoming less and less important as a source of gas, coal is heated in ovens or 'retorts'. A mixture of gases and volatile liquids is driven off, leaving coke behind in the oven. This coke is either used as a fuel or for reducing iron ores in the manufacture of steel.

When the hot gases coming from the oven cool down in condensers, coal tar liquefies and runs off into tar wells. This tar is a mixture which can be separated into a large number of useful chemicals, for example phenol, which can be used as an antiseptic and from which various plastics can be made.

Water is sprayed through the gas to remove ammonia, which is used to make fertilizers. A light oil also separates, containing a high proportion of benzene and toluene. These two chemicals are very useful as solvents and as starting materials for making lots of other, very useful substances.

Hydrogen sulphide gas, also present, would be a nuisance if it was left in because it forms a strongly acidic oxide when it is burned. So it is removed, too. The sulphur it contains is used to make sulphuric acid.

Gas

A coal carbonisation plant. (London News Agency)

Figure 52 gives some idea of the wide range of useful things which are by-products of this method of making town gas.

(ii) Gasification methods
These are newer processes in which coal or oil are completely turned into gas.

Oil refineries can supply the gas industry with large quantities of a low boiling liquid called 'naphtha'. This is a mixture of hydrocarbons with molecules ranging from five carbon atoms and twelve hydrogen up to ones with twelve of carbon and twenty-six of hydrogen. To change this liquid to a gas, the Gas Board have to break these molecules into smaller ones containing not more than four carbon atoms and ten hydrogen atoms.

They have several ways of doing this, but an important stage that occurs in each method is one in which naphtha vapour and steam are passed, at a high temperature, over a special substance (called a 'catalyst') which helps the reaction but does not get used up in it. This gives either a gas rich in hydrocarbons which produce a lot of heat when they burn, or mainly hydrogen—depending on the temperature and proportions of naphtha vapour and steam used. Volume for volume, hydrogen gives less heat when it is burned than hydrocarbons do, so it is called a 'lean' gas. However, it can be heated with more naphtha vapour to produce a 'rich' gas.

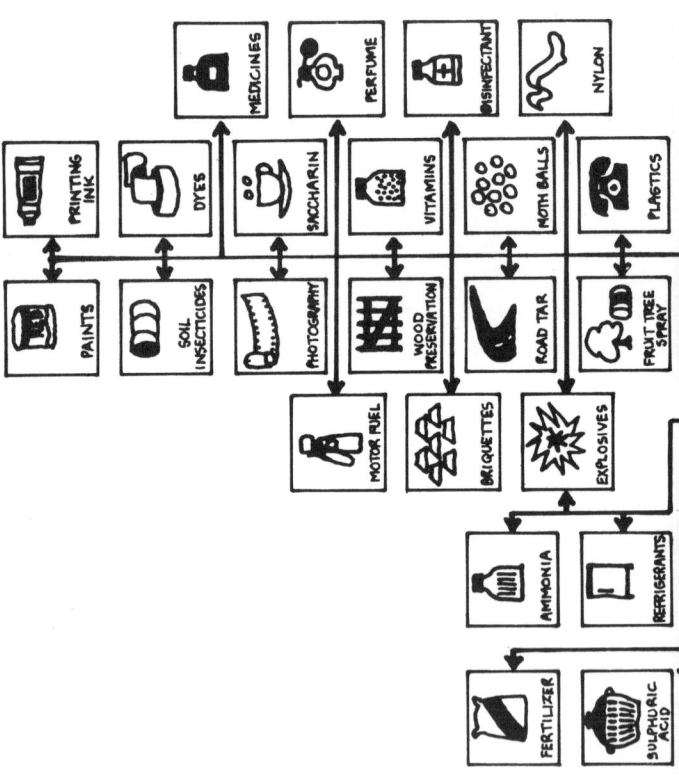

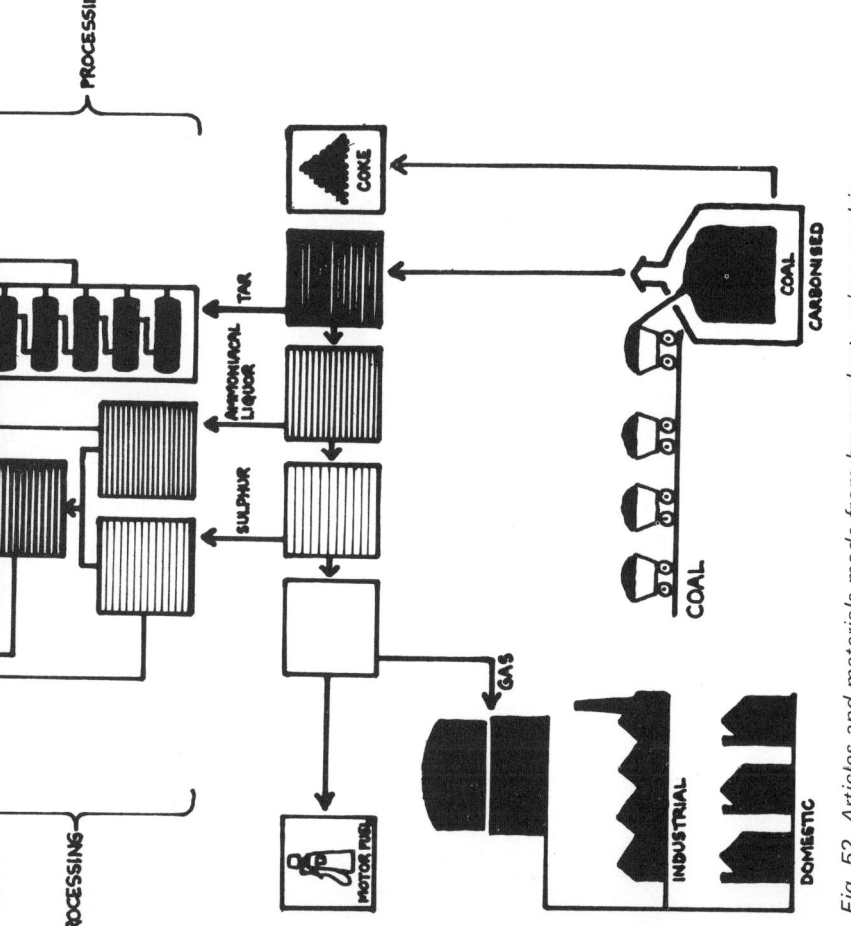

Fig. 52 Articles and materials made from by-products when coal is carbonised to coke and gas.

(iii) Natural gas

The biggest change in the gas industry is in the introduction and increasing use of 'natural gas'. Natural gas is a mixture of hydrocarbon gases, usually more than nine-tenths of it being methane (the 'firedamp' of coal mines).

It occurs with crude oil trapped below ground, underneath folds of impermeable rock. The methods of looking for folds of rock likely to be holding natural gas are the ones I described in Chapter 9, for oil.

View of part of the natural gas field at Hassi R'Mel in the Sahara Desert from where gas is piped to Arzew. Methane has been separated from other substances in the natural gas. The flammable impurities are being burned in the flares. (Courtesy of the Gas Council)

A view of part of CAMEL'S liquefaction plant at Arzew. In the background can be seen the 6,000 ton storage tanks, the jetty and one of the tankers. (Gas Council)

There is a huge natural gas field at Hassi R'Mel in Algeria. The gas is piped to the port of Arzew on the shore of the Mediterranean. There it is cooled and liquefied at a temperature of $-160°C$ (113 K). Two special tankers, the Methane Princess and the Methane Progress, bring 12,000 tons at a time of this liquefied gas to Britain and discharge it at a storage terminal at Canvey Island. There it is allowed to become gas again and is piped to various gas boards.

Starting in 1962, several major oil companies and the Gas Council made a seismic survey of the North Sea. They found large areas very deep down, in which the strata had promising domes of impermeable rock which could easily be holding oil or gas trapped under them.

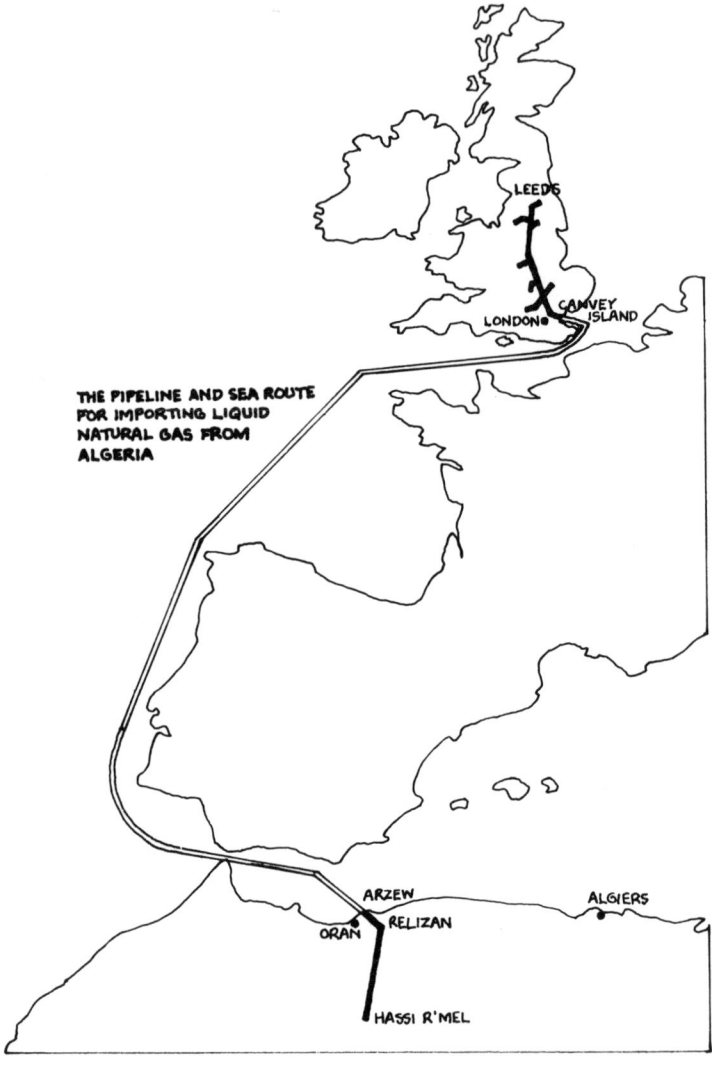

Fig. 53 The pipelines and sea route for importing liquid natural gas from Algeria.

A length of 36 inch diameter, high-pressure pipe being lowered into a trench during the laying of one of the Gas Council's feeder mains to transmit North Sea gas into the national distribution system. (Gas Council)

DRILLING THE BED OF THE NORTH SEA

Finding promising structures is one thing; you still have to drill to find out if they do in fact contain anything. Drilling the bed of the North Sea meant using special rigs: floating platforms which could be towed into position with their legs sticking up in the air. When over the required spot the legs were lowered to the sea floor and the platform was then jacked high above the water. For example, the 'Orion' can work in water up to 275 feet (82.5 m) deep, with waves running 64 feet (19 m) high, in winds up to 115 m.p.h. It can house a crew of 49 and drill a hole 20,000 feet (6,000 m) deep.

The British Petroleum Company struck the first large amount of gas, in 1965, at West Sole. Since 1967 an undersea pipeline from West Sole to Easington on the Yorkshire coast has supplied natural gas to the Gas Council. Three other large gas fields have been found under the North Sea:

Shock waves from this seismic explosion help reveal the pattern of the underlying strata. (Gas Council)

A drilling platform for drilling in the North Sea. (Courtesy of the Gas Council)

Indefatigable, Leman Bank and Hewett. It looks as if the bed of the North Sea can supply 3,000 million cubic feet (81 million cubic metres) of natural gas a day (three times the present day output of the entire British gas industry) for the next 30 years.

HOW CAN NATURAL GAS BE STORED TILL IT IS NEEDED?

One way of storing natural gas so that it can maintain a steady supply of gas is to pump it underground into a layer of porous rock. There are places in this country where folds of porous, waterlogged sandstone are covered over by an impermeable layer of clay (Figure 54). This is the right sort of structure in which to find a natural gas field, but they do not happen to contain any gas.

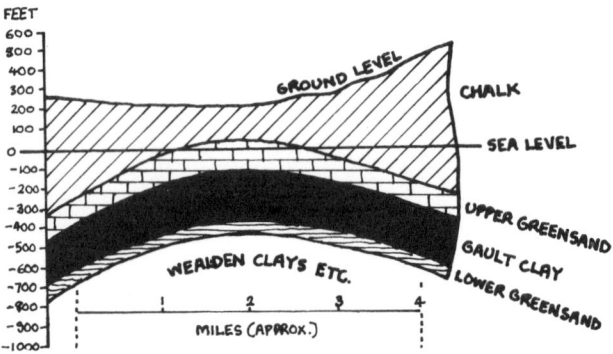

Fig. 54 A fold of porous, water-logged sandstone (lower greensand) covered with impermeable gault caly.

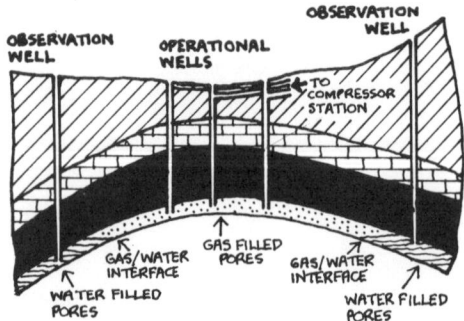

Fig. 55 How a suitable fold may be adapted as an underground store for natural gas.

Gas 133

If the gas obtained from the North Sea is pumped down into the porous sandstone layer, it drives the water further down. The gas is then trapped above the water and under the clay (Figure 55). It can then be drawn off steadily as required.

Another way of storing natural gas is to liquefy it since it takes up a much smaller space as a liquid than it does as a gas.

Natural gas is being stored as a liquid at Canvey Island, in large, cylindrical holes dug in the ground and covered by a gas-tight lid (Figure 56). Since liquid methane boils at −160 C (113 K), the earth sides and base of the holes are frozen hard so they will not collapse, or allow the liquid to soak away. This type of storage can be used to meet sudden demands for gas.

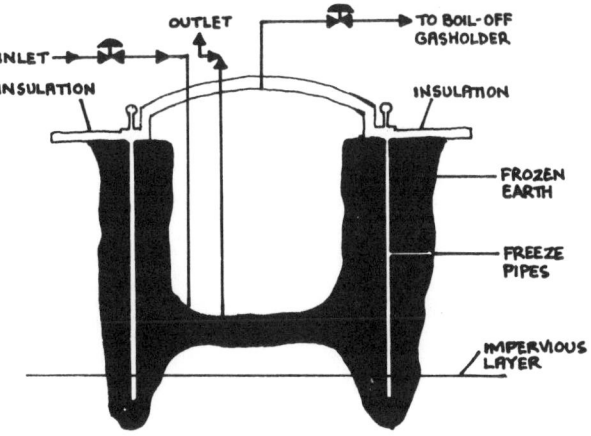

Fig. 56 Diagrammatic section of an underground storage tank for liquefied natural gas.

Fire and Fuels

A frozen ground storage unit for liquefied natural gas from Algeria, installed for the Gas Council at the Canvey Island Terminal. 130 feet (39 m) in diameter and 130 feet deep, this unit will store liquid methane at $-161\,°C$ (112K). It can hold an average day's gas supply for the whole of Britain. (Courtesy of the Gas Council)

A BURNING PROBLEM

The composition of coal gas varies but it is roughly one half hydrogen and one third methane (the rest is made up of various other gases). Natural gas is almost pure methane. Methane burns more slowly than hydrogen and needs four times as much oxygen (hence four times as much air) (see Figure 57). This means that natural gas burns more slowly than coal gas and needs much more air in which to do it.

Most gas burners in this country have been designed to burn coal gas (Figure 58(a)). If they are supplied with natural gas instead, the methane burns with a smoky yellow flame because it cannot get enough air, and it does not provide all the heat possible. To mix the gas with more air the gas injector hole must be made smaller and the gas pressure increased. This drags more air into the stream of gases going into the

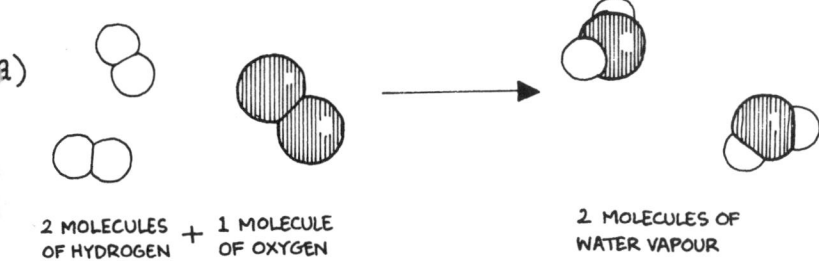

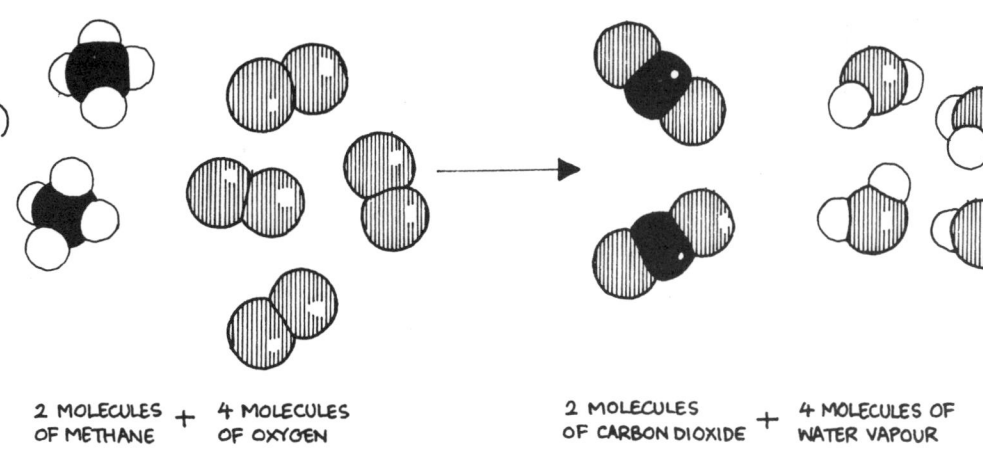

Fig. 57 What happens when (a) hydrogen and (b) methane are burnt in air.

burner ring. The trouble now is that, because methane burns comparatively slowly, the flame tends to lift off the burner (Figure 58(b)) and may well go out, blowing itself out in effect. To get over this extra holes are made in the burner so that some of the gas mixture comes out sufficiently slowly to burn steadily right where it comes out. This extra flame (called a 'retention' flame) stabilises the main flame and keeps it alight (Figure 58(c)).

It is obviously better to change or convert gas burners to natural gas burning rather than keep on making up mixtures of gases which burn like the old, fast disappearing, coal gas used to. So the Gas Council is changing domestic and industrial gas burners throughout the country, one section at a time, to natural gas burning. The total cost of this operation,

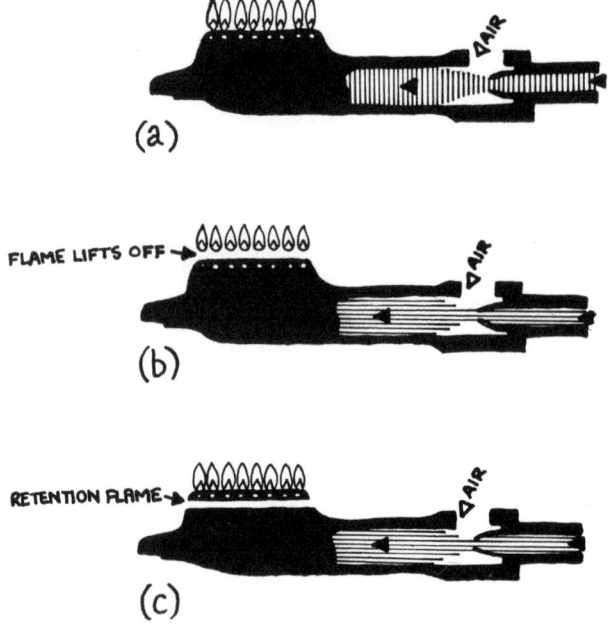

Fig. 58 (a) Town gas burner in operation. (b) Effect of burning natural gas in a town gas burner. (c) Modified burner for use with natural gas.

including laying the extra pipelines needed, may well amount to £600 million. This is being paid out by the gas industry. However they will recover it eventually because they will no longer need to process gas to make it like the old 'town gas'. Also natural gas contains twice as much energy as town gas so the Gas Council will be able to cope with increasing demands without having to begin an expensive programme of laying additional mains.

THINGS TO DO

You could write to the Public Relations Department of the Gas Council, 59, Bryanston Street, Marble Arch, London, W1A 2AZ, for their film catalogue and their current publications about the gas industry.

You could try to arrange a visit to your nearest gas works, or the Canvey Island terminal. To do this, get in touch with your local area gas board. This sort of visit is easier to arrange through a school or club, rather than by individuals.

11 ELECTRICITY

You may wonder what electricity has to do with fire and fuels? We certainly get heat from an electric fire and light from a bulb when we switch on the current—but there are no flames and nothing is burnt up.

WHERE DOES THE ELECTRICITY SUPPLY COME FROM?

If you spin a magnet inside a coil of wire, an electric current flows through the wire. This is the principle on which a bicycle dynamo works. If you try turning a bicycle dynamo with your fingers you will feel a resistance which uses up some of your energy. The energy needed to turn the dynamo against this resistance is changed to electrical energy. You can generate enough electricity for your bicycle lights by putting more effort into your pedalling.

Power stations use the same principle to produce the nation's electricity. The magnet used is a large electromagnet called a 'rotor'. A turbine (generally a steam driven one) turns the rotor and supplies the energy which the dynamo changes to electricity.

Steam turbines

In a power station, steam to drive the turbines is obtained either by using nuclear energy or by burning coal or oil to heat water. This is the stage at which we can see that electricity comes from the burning of a fuel. When we switch on the current at home we are taking advantage of fuel being burned a long way away.

Figure 59 shows the layout and working of a typical steam turbine.

High pressure steam passes through a ring of stationary blades fixed to the wall of the high pressure cylinder. These blades direct the steam, at an angle, on to a second ring of propellor blades fixed to the main shaft. This makes the shaft turn. In the diagram (Figure 59) this process happens four more times.

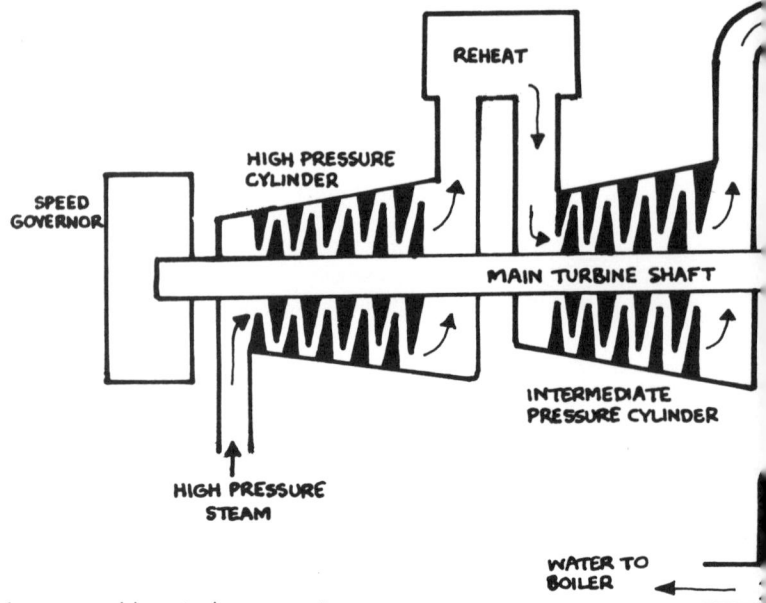

Fig. 59 Diagram of a steam-driven turbo-generator.

When the steam emerges from the cylinder, its pressure is lower and some of its heat has been changed to mechanical energy in turning the turbine.

After being reheated, the steam enters another cylinder at a lower pressure and more heat is changed into mechanical energy.

To get as much energy from the steam as possible it is now passed to the centre of a low pressure cylinder where it flows outwards through more rows of turbine blades. Cold water from cooling towers or a river or the sea flows through lots of pipes in the condenser. This makes the steam condense. The water so formed is fed back to the boiler again.

The speed governor keeps the main shaft rotating steadily at 50 turns a second—the same as the standard frequency of the alternating electric current produced by the generator. It controls the speed of the shaft by regulating the supply of high-pressure steam to the turbine.

A characteristic feature of coal-fired power stations is the big stockpile of coal required. Large machinery is needed to build up the pile and to supply coal to the boiler house. To keep down the cost of transporting

Electricity 139

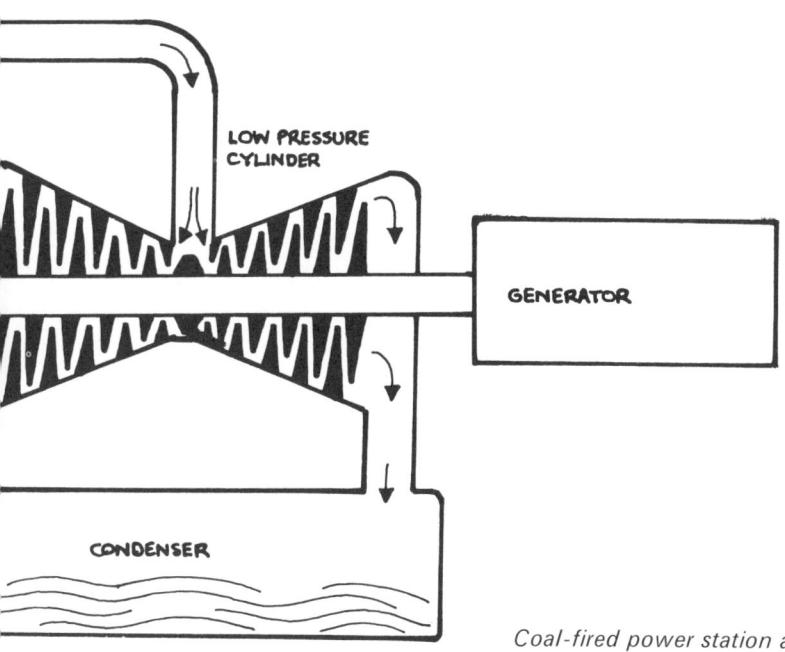

Coal-fired power station at Dunham-on-Trent, Nottinghamshire. (Courtesy of the Central Electricity Generating Board)

Giant machine for stockpiling coal and collecting it from stock, at Aberthaw power station. The nine buckets on the wheel can each hold almost one ton of coal. (Courtesy of the Central Electricity Generating Board)

coal, many power stations have been built on coal fields. Coal for the others is delivered either by ship or by train. Coal for the newest power stations is served by special 'merry-go-round' trains, so called because they go from colliery to power station and back without stopping.

At the colliery the train passes slowly under a bunker which fills each hopper in turn with coal. At the power station the hoppers shoot their loads into coal bunkers beneath the rails. Then, back the train goes and the whole cycle is repeated.

Electricity 141

The hoppers of a 'merry-go-round' train being filled from a colliery bunker. (Coal News)

Power stations producing the same amount of electricity can run more cheaply on oil than on coal. So, oil-burning power stations are being built beside the oil refineries in Britain: this saves the cost of carrying fuel oil.

The most obvious differences between oil-fired and coal-fired power stations are that the oil-fired ones do not have a large stockpile of coal nearby and that piping oil is a cleaner job than moving coal.

In some power stations the water is heated to produce steam, by nuclear energy. There is no fire here, and 'fuel' has a different meaning when applied to the uranium which produces the energy.

The fuel oil pipeline serving Kingsnorth oil-fired power station. (Aerofilms Ltd.)

A gas turbine at Croydon B power station. (Courtesy of the Central Electricity Generating Board)

Gas turbines

Another way of driving a turbine is with a high-pressure blast of hot exhaust gases. There are several power stations which burn gas. The big advantage of a gas turbo-generator is that it can be brought up to full power in a few seconds just by increasing the supply of gas, so it can cope with a sudden increase in demand in an emergency. By contrast, there is always a slight delay with steam turbines between increasing the rate of burning of coal or oil, and an increase in steam pressure.

Nuclear Power

How does a nuclear power station work? A nuclear power station is very much like a coal- or oil-fired one. In all power stations steam turbines drive generators, which produce electricity. The difference between the three kinds is in the way in which the water is heated to produce high-pressure steam. In coal- and oil-fired power stations the heat is obtained by burning a fuel, whereas in a nuclear power station no burning occurs and the source of energy is completely different.

Where does nuclear energy come from? We are already familiar with the idea of atoms being the small particles of elements which take part in chemical reactions like burning, for example. In the first 30 years of this century it became clear that these atoms are themselves composed of a number of still smaller particles. The three main building blocks of which all atoms are made are protons, neutrons and electrons.

Protons and neutrons have the same mass (about the same as that of a hydrogen atom), but differ in that a proton has a positive electrical charge while a neutron is electrically neutral. Electrons are very much lighter than protons and neutrons and carry a negative electrical charge the same size as that on a proton.

	Mass	Electric Charge
Proton	About the same as a hydrogen atom	Positive
Neutron	About the same as a hydrogen atom	Neutral
Electron	Much lighter	Negative (same size as proton's)

Electricity

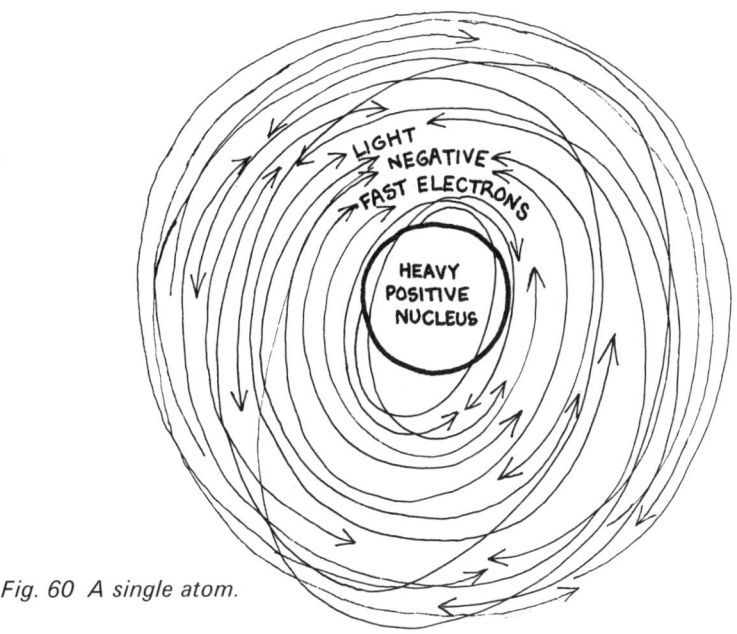

Fig. 60 A single atom.

Each atom has a tiny, positively charged nucleus in the middle. This nucleus carries most of the mass of the atom. The space round the mucleus, which the atom occupies, is filled by the very light, fast-moving, negatively charged electrons (see Figure 60).

The nuclei of atoms are made up of protons and neutrons. The attraction of the positive protons keeps the atom's negative electrons close to it. The atoms of each element have their own particular number of protons in each of their nuclei. The number of neutrons can vary.

Not all atomic nuclei are equally stable: some have more energy than others. The nuclei of a kind of uranium called uranium-235 are less stable than most. If a uranium-235 nucleus is hit by a slow-moving neutron, it breaks into two, forming two more stable nuclei. At the same time, it shoots out two or three fast neutrons and gives out an enormous amount of energy. This process is called nuclear fission (Figure 61).

The fast neutrons are emitted at speeds of thousands of miles per second. If they are slowed down to about a mile a second (or less) they are able to split other uranium-235 nuclei—if they hit them.

Fig. 61 Nuclear fission.

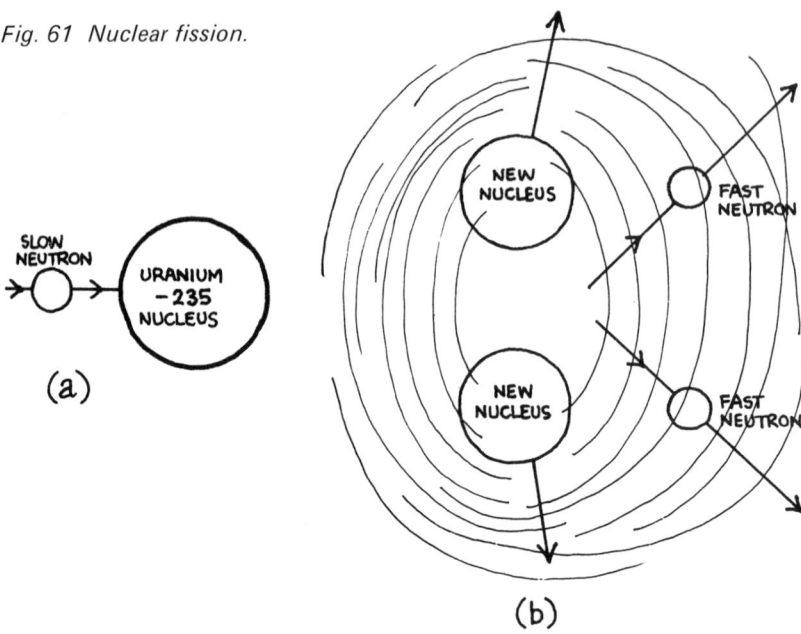

If every fission produced two neutrons, think what would happen if each neutron caused a further fission—and so on.

      1 fission would lead to 2 more fissions,
these 2 fissions would lead to 2×2 more,
these 4 fissions would lead to 4×2 more,
these 8 fissions would lead to 8×2 more, and so on.

Thus the process is accelerating and getting out of control.

Now these fissions can take place in less than a millionth of a second and each one is accompanied by the release of a lot of energy so, unless the process is controlled in some way, we have a violent explosion (an atomic bomb).

In a nuclear power station these fission reactions are controlled. Some of the neutrons are absorbed before they can cause further fissions. The energy liberated by the fissions that do take place is used to turn water into high-pressure steam to drive the turbo-generators.

FURTHER READING

The Public Relations Branch of the Central Electricity Generating Board, (Sudbury House, 15 Newgate St. London E.C.1) produce interesting booklets with very good colour diagrams called 'How Electricity is Made and Transmitted'; 'Network for the Nation'; and 'Power Controlled'.

They also have a film library and will supply a catalogue if asked.

The Marketing Department of the Electricity Council, 30, Millbank, London, S.W.1, produce a booklet entitled 'Electricity and You'. They also supply a catalogue of films.

Both of these bodies would rather be approached by schools than by lots of individuals, in order to keep their correspondence within reasonable limits.

THINGS TO DO

Try to arrange a visit to your nearest power station. This is something better done as an organised party, e.g. members of a school, than as an individual.

BOOKS TO READ

The Silent Energy, Philip Kogan and Joan Pick (Lampson Low, Marston & Co., London, 1966).
The Story of Nuclear Power, E. H. Childs, Ladybird Books (Wills & Hepworth, 1972).
Power Stations Work Like This, Rolt Hammond (Phoenix, 1960).
Power From the Sun, The Story of Solar Energy, D. S. Halacy (John Murray, 1972).
Energy and Power, Chapter 7, 'Atomic Energy', Albert Hinkelbein (Collins, 1971).

12 FIRE, THE BAD MASTER

So far we have looked at ways of producing fire and using it for our own purposes; fire makes a good servant. On the other hand, fire out of control proves to be dangerous and costly; this is why it is said to be a bad master. Because it is so dangerous when it gets out of hand, about making shops, offices, factories, schools, cinemas and other places to make it difficult for a fire to spread if it does break out.

There are laws which compel employers to take reasonable precautions. They must provide fire extinguishers, fire escapes and fireproof doors and control the way in which flammable materials are stored and used. All fire brigades, insurance companies and some businesses will give advice about making shops, offices, schools, cinemas and other places of entertainment as safe as possible from fires.

Every year, thousands of people are killed or injured by accidental fires in their homes. Your parents are responsible for your home being safe, but you can play your part and help them keep it safe.

HOW CAN WE REDUCE THE RISK OF FIRE AT HOME?

If you have an open coal fire in your home, make sure there is a proper fire guard fixed in place, enclosing the fire at the front, sides and top. Airing clothes on the fire guard is a common cause of fires. If you find clothes on the fire guard, point out the danger in a tactful way.

Portable electric and gas fires and oil heaters are dangerous because they can be moved so easily. They should never be carried while alight or switched on; you should try to point out the danger of dropping it, if you see one being carried.

This badly burned door was closed during the fire. You can see that it kept the fire out so that the room is practically undamaged.
(London Fire Brigade photo)

Oil heaters should never be left in a draught because it can make them flare up dangerously. Make sure they are never placed near furniture or bedding, because they could easily set light to them. Do not play near a portable fire or heater because you or your friends could easily knock it over.

The best place for heaters and fires is in the fireplace, protected with a fire guard. The chimney opening behind an oil heater should be reduced with a non-combustible screen so that it is no larger than 20 square inches. It also important to keep oil heaters standing level.

Polystrene cement, balsa cement, model aircraft dopes and lots of aerosols have flammable vapours. Do not use them near a fire because the vapour-laden air could easily ignite with a flash.

Get rid of oily rags after you have cleaned your bicycle. Air can slowly oxidise the oil and grease in them. If they are bundled together, the heat produced does not escape so the bundle grows hotter and hotter until it eventually bursts into flames.

Things to remember on the fifth of November

The fifth of November, Bonfire Night, is always a busy night for fire brigades—and a sad night in many homes and hospitals, too. Every year children are burned, many of them seriously, because fireworks are carelessly handled. Although your parents are responsible for your safety on Bonfire Night, you can help them by keeping the following simple rules and encouraging them, tactfully, to observe them, too.

Do keep fireworks in a closed tin—well away from bonfires.
Do follow the instructions printed on the fireworks.
Don't throw fireworks.
Don't touch a firework which doesn't go off, for at least 10 minutes.
Build bonfires well away from houses, fences and sheds. Lay out a garden hose or keep a bucket of water handy in case it looks like getting out of hand.
Above all, never try to revive a bonfire with petrol or paraffin.

WHAT SHOULD WE DO IF A FIRE BREAKS OUT?

Now you know some of the ways in which you can help prevent accidental fires. But accidents do happen. Do you know what to do if you find fire has broken out?

The first and most important thing to do is raise the alarm. Don't take risks and don't waste time trying to put it out. Yell 'FIRE!'. Make lots of noise and warn everybody in the house so they can get out.

As you go out, close all the doors behind you. This makes it harder for the fire to get the air it needs and prevents burning gases spreading to other rooms. An ordinary door can hold back fire for as much as twenty minutes.

Call the Fire Brigade. To do this, first find a telephone and dial '999'. This emergency call is answered by the Post Office telephone exchange. The operator will ask for the number from which you are speaking. (It is written in the middle of the dial.) This means you can be traced if you give an incomplete address or if the message gets broken off. You will then be given a choice of 'Police, Fire or Ambulance'. In this case you choose 'Fire', of course. The telephone operator immediately puts your call through to the Fire Brigade Headquarters and listens in to make sure it is properly connected. Then you give the address of the fire and any other information you can. Keep calm and make your message as helpful as possible.

After that, you have done all you reasonably can. Leave the actual fire fighting to grown-ups unless you have had a proper course in it, as a Boy Scout or Girl Guide or as part of the Duke of Edinburgh's Award Scheme, for instance.

What to do if trapped!
If you have had the bad luck to be trapped in an upstairs room because of a fire outside, you can improve your chances a lot by keeping calm and thinking clearly. For a start, shut the door and stop smoke coming through the gap at the bottom by sealing it with a blanket or rug. Then go to the window, open it a little at the top and bottom and breathe fresh air at the lower opening. Smoke will leave by the top opening. You should shout for help as loudly as you can. Only jump as a last resort.
If help does not come and you cannot stay any longer don't just jump. Climb out of the window and hang down by your fingertips before dropping. This can shorten the distance you have to fall by five or six feet. If you are on the second floor or above, jumping is dangerous and I hope you never have to do it.

The Central Brigade Control Room which receives emergency calls in the Inner London area.
You can see: The map which shows the appliances available at stations throughout the G.L.C. area. To its right is a board showing which officers are available and how they can be reached. The 'Fire Situation' board on the left gives the address of each fire and shows what appliances are attending to it: each pale-coloured symbol represents one machine of some sort; and each black one indicates that the 'stop' message has been received. The number of fires shown on the board is unusually large because it is Guy Fawkes night. The girls wearing headphones are the telephone operators receiving emergency calls. On the left of the picture are the rotary drums carrying street index cards. (London Fire Brigade photo)

Fire, the bad master   153

What happens when you have called the Fire Brigade?
Although the general action is always similar, the details of what happens to your message vary slightly from one area to the next. I shall describe what happens in the Inner London area.

All calls go straight to the central Brigade Control. Here, one operator takes the message while another one who is listening in identifies the address from a street index card—one of thousands mounted on rotary drums for quick reference. Every street has a card on the drum, giving details of what appliances should be sent to any fire there to begin with. The card also says where the nearest fire station is which can supply them. It also lists other fire stations to be called on next if the appliances at the first station are already out somewhere else.

The operator now pushes switches which connect up a teleprinter system to the fire station or stations chosen (this automatically rings the station's call bells) and sends a teleprinter message about the fire. The station teleprinter produces several copies of the message, giving the address of the fire, and one of these is taken by the officer in charge of each appliance. At the same time another copy goes to the Headquarters of the London Salvage Corps, a body sponsored by the insurance companies, who will do what they can to protect anything of value from the effects of fire.

In the Inner London area, the Fire Brigade set themselves a limit of five minutes between receiving a call and starting to fight the fire. They always manage to get there within the time.

Control is in two-way radio contact with the appliances which go out so that extra help can be called up quickly, if necessary. When the officer in charge at the fire decides he has sufficient help to cope with the fire he sends a 'stop' message to Control by radio. This tells Control that they need not arrange for any more reinforcements.

In this way the Central Control can deal with more than one large fire or other incident at the same time and there is no danger of calls for help going to a fire station which is empty because all its appliances are already out at a fire.

How are fires put out?
There are three general ways of putting out a fire. These are: starving it by cutting off the supply of fuel; suffocating it by keeping out its

Turntable ladder being used to rescue people trapped by fire.

supply of oxygen; and cooling it down till it can no longer burn.

There are three main types of fire with their own special dangers, which need slightly different methods of putting them out.

First, there is the type in which wood, paper, fabric or similar material is burning. This type can be put out by cooling and shutting air out with a lot of water, or by squirting on it a foam of soda-acid. 'Soda-acid' fire extinguishers contain a solution of washing soda and a bottle of acid. To work them you have to break the bottle of acid

Fighting a fire in a timberyard. (London Fire Brigade photo)

either by hitting a knob on the extinguisher or by turning it upside down and banging it on the ground. The soda and acid produce a lot of foam made of millions of bubbles of carbon dioxide. This covers the fire and shuts out the supply of oxygen from the air.

The second type of fire is due to a burning liquid like petrol, oil or cooking fat. It is no good putting water on these because the burning liquid will simply float on top and spread further. You could use a foam extinguisher again because the foam will cover the surface of the liquid. Another sort of extinguisher which can be used is the 'dry powder' sort. This blows a thick layer of fine bicarbonate of soda powder onto the burning liquid and blocks out the air. Also there are fire extinguishers which contain carbon dioxide under pressure. On pulling the trigger, these give a strong jet of carbon dioxide gas which blankets the fire and cools it.

The third type of fire is one started by an electrical apparatus overheating or short circuiting. In this case there is the danger of getting an electric shock when you try to put the fire out. Switch off the electric power before doing anything else. For safety, in case it is still 'live', use a non-conducting fire extinguisher. Dry powder or carbon dioxide will do. Water or soda-acid would be dangerous.

THINGS TO DO

You can be trained in fire prevention and fire fighting in the Boy Scouts or Girl Guides, or as a part of the Duke of Edinburgh's Award Scheme.

You can get information about and instruction in fire prevention from your local fire brigade. This is more conveniently arranged through school than individually. For example, the London Fire Brigade give film shows, lecture demonstrations and a look at the machines to school children at its headquarters early in January each year. At other times throughout the year organised school parties are shown round for general interest without instruction. Officers also give lecture demonstrations in schools in the area.

You could join the Fire Brigade Society. This is a society for people interested in anything to do with fire fighting. The General Secretary is

> Mr R. Bonner,
> 20, Chipping Street,
> Longsight,
> Manchester, M12 4LB.

BOOKS YOU CAN READ

Your local fire brigade probably issues a handbook which you could buy for a few pence. Write to the Chief Officer and ask.

London's Fire Brigades, W. E. Jackson (Longmans, 1966).
The Ladybird 'Easy Reading' book, *The Fireman,* Vera Southgate and J. Havenhand.

Fire, the bad master

Read the Science Museum Illustrated Booklet, *Fire Engines and Other Fire Fighting Appliances.*
The Fireman, J. Anderson; People's Jobs, E. S. A. Information Book.
Fire!, M. Neurath (Max Parrish, London, 1955).
The True Book About Fire-Fighting, E. Larsen (Frederick Muller Ltd., London, 1962).
Fires and Firemen, H. Adams, Blackwell's Learning Library, No. 1 (Basil Blackwell, 1961).
Fire Alarm, Paul C. Ditzel (Van Nostrand Reinhold, 1969).
Fire, Leonard Rule, A New Citizen Book (Wayland, 1973).

13 THE GREAT FIRE OF LONDON

At the time of the fire, streets of houses like these were a common feature of the City of London. (Photo by R. B. Fleming & Co., Ltd., of material at the Guildhall)

The great fire of London

Pudding Lane in the City of London used to be a narrow, cobbled street which ran down towards the river Thames at Fish Wharf. Each side was lined by a row of tumbledown Tudor buildings. Each storey overhung the one underneath so that the buildings on either side leaned towards each other over the road. Very little sunlight could find its way down into the street with its smelly open sewer running down the middle. In hundreds of unhealthy little streets like these, vermin and disease abounded. Epidemics of bubonic plague broke out from time to time, spread by fleas carrying the bacillus, who lived on the rats which infested these houses. The buildings in Pudding Lane were made largely from wood and were coated with pitch to keep out the wind and rain.

HOW THE FIRE STARTED

Thomas Farynor, the King's baker, lived with his daughter and two servants above his bakehouse there. Some time between midnight and two in the morning of Sunday, 2 September 1666, his stack of firewood for the oven caught fire and the flames spread to the rest of the ground floor. The smell of smoke roused the sleeping household. Unable to escape through the ground floor, they were forced to climb to the top of the house. Thomas Farynor, his daughter Hannah and his manservant climbed out of a window on to the roof and escaped to the house next door. The maid was too frightened of the drop to the road below to follow them. Instead, she stayed at the window until she was killed as the burning house collapsed.

WHY THE FIRE SPREAD

In those days there was no proper fire brigade. People did what they could to protect their property, with buckets of water, and moved their belongings into the street for safety. Usually a fire like this would burn down one group of buildings but could be stopped from spreading further. Three factors combined to make this fire an exception: (1) a long drought had thoroughly dried out the pitch-coated timber buildings; (2) the city's wharves and warehouses, packed with flammable stocks of wood, coal, oil, butter and sugar, were nearby on the banks of the Thames and (3) after 2 a.m., a strong wind got up from the north-east, fanning the flames and carrying sparks to buildings beyond the fire. Sparks set fire to piles of hay and straw in the yard of the Star Inn in the next street to the west, Fish Street Hill. Soon, the whole of the wooden inn blazed up.

An artist's impression of the fire of London at its height. (London Museum photo)

The Lord Mayor of London, Sir Thomas Bludworth, came to look at the fire just after 3 o'clock in the morning and decided it was not important. Later in the day, as the wind grew stronger, he realised he was wrong. He organised chains of people to pass buckets of water from hand to hand to the fires.

Some city companies and parishes owned private fire engines. By the time their owners had given permission for these engines to be used, the fire was burning too fiercely to be controlled. These engines were practically

The great fire of London

Map of the area devastated by the fire of London. (Photo by R. B. Fleming & Co., Ltd., of material at the Guildhall)

useless, anyway, because the roads and alleys were too narrow and were piled high with furniture and belongings brought out of the houses.

The only hope of holding the fire now was to pull down rows of houses and clear spaces which the fire could not cross. The Lord Mayor was reluctant to order this because, according to the law, if you destroyed someone's house you had to pay for it to be rebuilt.

So the fire spread.

After midday on that Sunday, people did begin to pull down houses but they started work too close to the fire. The houses on which they were working burst into flames before they could be torn down.

Water for the City was supplied by giant water wheels under the arches of London Bridge. These forced water into wooden and lead pipes which carried it round the City.

Usually when a fire broke out, people punched holes in the pipes and drew off water to put it out. However, this fire spread to London Bridge and burned wooden houses on the northern part of the Bridge. At the same time it put the water wheels out of action so that the pipes ran dry.

Three times as much of London burned on Monday as on Sunday. By the end of Tuesday practically the whole of the ancient City of London had been destroyed. St. Paul's Cathedral and Newgate prison and gateway were burned; the Tower of London was the only famous old building which was saved. It had to be, as it contained enough gunpowder to blow up London Bridge and ships in the Thames, and start the fire off again beyond the city wall. Houses in Tower Street were blown up with gunpowder to make a big fire-break to save the Tower.

HOW THE FIRE ENDED

At 11 o'clock on Tuesday night the wind swung round to the south and dropped. The thick walls of St. Dunstan's in Fleet Street and the Temple Church were now sufficient to stop the fire spreading further west. By Wednesday morning the fire was about all over. There was one more outbreak in the afternoon, in a building near the Temple. Some buildings were blown up to prevent it setting light to the Temple Church and Hall. On Thursday morning the fire was out.

Of the 450 acres within the walls of the City, five-sixths were destroyed. Another 63 acres outside the wall were devastated too; 89 parish churches and 13,200 houses were burnt together with more than 50 of the City Companies' Halls, 3 city gates, 4 stone bridges and the prisons of Newgate, the Fleet, and the Poultry and Wood Street Compters.

In spite of all this destruction, only about half a dozen people were killed directly by the fire. The inhabitants all had time to leave their homes and push their way, with what belongings they could carry, through the

The great fire of London

streets out into the open country. Thousands of Londoners roughed it in fields and open ground all round the City. There, the villagers took them into their own houses so that the fields were virtually empty again by the end of the week.

The fire of London provided a splendid opportunity to build a better city. The destruction of the old city, with its narrow streets and wooden buildings, made possible the building of a new city with broad roads, open spaces and stone buildings of regulated heights. A Rebuilding Act was passed in 1667, designed to lessen the fire risks and to make London a cleaner, healthier city. Streets were widened and open sewers gave way to covered ones. All building was controlled. Wooden houses were banned and overhanging gables were not allowed. Anyone who built a house which did not conform with the regulations had it pulled down again.

Sir Christopher Wren was made Surveyor General and Principal Architect for rebuilding the whole city. He designed many of the splendid new buildings, including the new St. Paul's Cathedral. He also designed the Monument to commemorate the fire, which stands on the site of St. Margaret, Fish Street Hill, where the first church was destroyed in the fire. It is a pillar 202 feet (60.6 m) high and 130 feet (39 m) from the bakery where it all began.

THINGS YOU CAN DO

Visit the London Museum, Kensington Palace, London, W8. They have a good collection of paintings, engravings and books about the Great Fire.

Climb the Monument and enjoy the view from the platform at the top. Read the inscription on the base and the guide book. Try to find the spot where the fire started.

Many towns have had a big fire at some time or other in their history. Try local history and guide books to see if there was one where you live. If it happened within the last 80 years the files of your local newspaper may well give the details.

Questions to keep in mind: Where did it start? How? When? How and why did it spread? Are there traces remaining? What improvements (if any) resulted from it?

READING

John Dryden wrote a historical poem called 'Annus Mirabilis' (The Year of Wonders), in which there is a description of the Great Fire (as well as battles with the Dutch).

Samuel Pepys was in London during the Great Fire and he gives a moving, eye-witness account of it in his Diary.

The Plague and the Fire of London, Mollie and Michael Hardwick (Max Parrish, London).
Look at the 'Jackdaw' No. 2, *The Plague and Fire of London,* compiled and edited by John Langdon-Davies (Jonathan Cape, 30, Bedford Square, London, W.C.1.).
London and the Great Fire, John E. N. Hearsay (Murray, 1969).
The Elements Series, Book 2, *Fire,* Bernard Henry, Chapter 4, 'Fire the Destroyer' (John Kaker, 1968).

14 FIRE IN WAR

PROPELLANTS AND EXPLOSIVES

Firing a gun involves burning a propellant such as gunpowder or cordite. It is a very quick sort of burning but, as we described in Chapter 7, it is burning nonetheless. The hot gases produced under high pressure drive the bullet or shell up the barrel of the gun.

A bomb or shell explodes because an explosive inside it has burned very quickly, again producing hot gases under high pressure. This time they can only excape by bursting their container. The pressure then released is capable of doing further severe damage to anything in its way.

However, this is not the only way in which fire is or has been used in war. As soon as they had begun to control fire, simple tribes probably used it against their enemies—smoking them out of their caves, burning their huts or shelters, or driving them before a belt of fire fanned by the wind. To these simple methods they added, by degrees, flaming arrows, fire pots, blazing pitch, naptha, sulphur and charcoal.

FLAME THROWERS

In AD 673, the Saracens were trying to capture Constantinople from the Greeks. An architect named Callinicus, who had fled from Heliopolis in Syria to Constantinople, prepared a secret weapon for his Greek hosts to use to defend their city. As the Saracen ships drew near, the Greeks aimed pipes at them from the bows of their galleys. Over the Saracens they squirted a liquid which caught fire as soon as it became wet and which could not be put out with water. The Saracen ships burned and the city of Constantinople was saved. This was the first battle in which flame throwers were used.

The composition of 'Greek Fire' was kept secret and now we can never know for sure how it was made. Possibly it was a mixture containing quicklime and oil. Quicklime grows very hot when it is moistened and could, perhaps, ignite some volatile oil. However it was made, it was the forerunner of the modern flame thrower.

An attack on a U-boat. The three large balls of light are flares dropped by a Sunderland aircraft to light the U-boat before the attack. The outline of the submarine can be seen in the swirling foam. (Imperial War Museum)

Fire in War

World War I: flame throwers in action against a British tank. (Imperial War Museum photo)

The Germans made and tested the first modern flame throwers at the beginning of this century. They were also the first to use them, in 1915, during World War I, as a surprise weapon against the Allies. Soon the British and French made their own. A modern flame thrower consists of one or more fuel tanks with one or more cylinders of compressed gas to squirt the fuel out, a flexible hose, a trigger nozzle and some means of lighting the jet of fuel.

In World War II a portable flame thrower was used which one man could carry on his back. This had a range of about 45 metres and could fire a continuous burst for ten seconds. In practice, several short bursts were more efficient and more economical than one long one. Tanks carried larger, heavier flame throwers which had a range of 100 metres and enough fuel to fire a continuous burst for 60 seconds. Flame throwers were one of the few weapons which could be used effectively against the Japanese soldiers who fought from caves and strong coconut log bunkers, on the Pacific Islands.

Modern British and United States' flame throwers are fuelled with 'Napalm', a thickened petrol which carries further than ordinary petrol, burns with

fire bombs fitted as wing tanks to fighter bombers in World War II and in the Korean War.

FIRE SHIPS

Greek Fire used against the Saracen ships was an early example of how fire can be used effectively in a sea battle. Another way which has been used for thousands of years is to float fireships into the enemy fleet. A fireship is a wooden ship packed with gunpowder, pitch or anything else that will burn readily. A small crew must sail it, towing another boat, close to the enemy. Then they set fire to it and escaped in the second boat while the fireship drifts into the enemy. It was most effective against fleets of wooden sailing ships at anchor, because until they had set sail and got under way they could not steer to avoid the burning hulks drifting into them.

How fire ships helped to defeat the Spanish Armada

The Armada set sail from Spain in order to escort the Duke of Parma's army across the Channel to attack the south-east corner of England. His army was supposed to embark at invasion ports in the Low Countries where it would not stand a chance against the English and Dutch fleets without massive support.

Sir Francis Drake was playing an after-dinner game of bowls on the Hoe when the 'Golden Hind' sailed into Plymouth Sound on Friday evening, 19th July 1588. Her captain, Thomas Flemyng, hurried up to tell him he had sighted the Spanish Armada.

Warning beacons were lit on hill tops to flash the news of their coming, across England. Howard and Drake's fleet put to sea that night. Beating against a south-west wind, they were off the Eddystone Rocks when they first saw the Spaniards, just after mid-day next day. A great crescent of Spanish ships was sailing up the Channel from the west, within sight of land.

Fireships being launched against the Spanish Armada off Calais. (Photo of an oil painting in the National Maritime Museum, by an unknown artist)

During the night that followed, Howard and Drake's fleet slipped round the enemy so that on the morning of Sunday, 21st July, they were to windward of the Spaniards and a little further out to sea. The English ships put about and sailed in to attack. The Spanish were at a disadvantage since they would have the wind against them if they turned to fight, and they would also no longer be advancing up the Channel. All that week the English ships harried the Spaniards as they moved up the Channel, but were unable to break their formation. By the end of the week their ammunition was running low.

At 5 p.m. on Saturday, 27th July, the Spanish ships anchored off Calais where they waited for Parma to embark his army at Dunkirk. If they had not stopped there, they would have run the risk of being driven right out into the North Sea.

The English fleet dropped anchor, too, still to windward. Just as it grew dark, more ships, under Lord Henry Seymour, joined the English fleet. These brought its strength up to 140 ships.

However, Parma was not ready to embark at Dunkirk.

All next day, while the Spaniards waited, the English were preparing eight fireships. At midnight they sailed, the wind and tide with them, into the anchored Armada. Taken by surprise, the Spaniards cut their cables so they could run with the wind and tide and keep clear of the blazing fireships. Although they dodged the fireships, the Spanish ships lost their tight, strong formation. During Monday, 29th July, 1588, the English fleet drove them slowly eastwards in the great battle of Gravelines, right beyond England into the North Sea. With the wind coming from the south-west, the Spanish ships could not turn back into the Channel to carry out their task of escorting an army against England.

We can only be sure that eleven Spanish ships were sunk during their run up the Channel—we lost none. The real defeat of the Spanish fleet only began when they were driven from their moorings at Calais in the middle of the night, by eight fireships.

The remnants of the Spanish Armada had to take the long way home, round Scotland and Ireland back to Spain. Weakened by hunger and battered by storms, the Spanish lost many more ships off our coasts so that the final score came to something between 50 and 60 ships and several thousand men.

INCENDIARY BOMBS AND FIRE RAIDS

Apart from high-explosive bombs, bombers during World War II carried metal incendiary bombs. One type was made mainly of magnesium—you probably know how strongly and brightly that burns!

On 14th November, 1940, the Germans dropped hundreds of incendiary bombs on Coventry and, as a result, the whole of the city centre was destroyed by fire. It was this raid which showed just how destructive an aerial fire raid could be, and led both sides to try to mount bigger and bigger raids of this sort.

In three night raids on Hamburg in July 1943, the Royal Air Force started fires over large areas. In particular, the second raid, on the night of 27th to 28th, caused lots of fires over 17 square miles (43 square kilometres) and made one area of over 5 square miles (13 square kilometres) of concentrated fire. Here, so many fires started that the flames all merged into one column. This produced so much heat that all the buildings

View of London dockland during the 1940 'blitz' fire raids. (London Fire Brigade photo)

underneath caught fire. This terrible effect is called a 'fire-storm'. It differed from ordinary conflagrations which spread along a path, giving the population a chance to retreat in front of it. In this fire storm, the whole area was ignited and its inhabitants were trapped. A similar fire raid on Dresden in 1945 caused a fire storm which dwarfed all previous attacks on German cities. This was towards the end of the war with Germany and no one had time to make a detailed record of the damage. We do know, though, that over 35,000 were killed.

SCORCHED-EARTH TACTICS

It is possible to defeat an enemy by burning even your own country (or the country you are helping to defend). Obviously this is a desperate measure since what you burn is lost to you as well as to the enemy.

At the battle of Talavera in July 1809, Wellesley's army successfully resisted an attack by a much larger French one. For this great feat of arms, Wellesley was made Viscount Wellington.

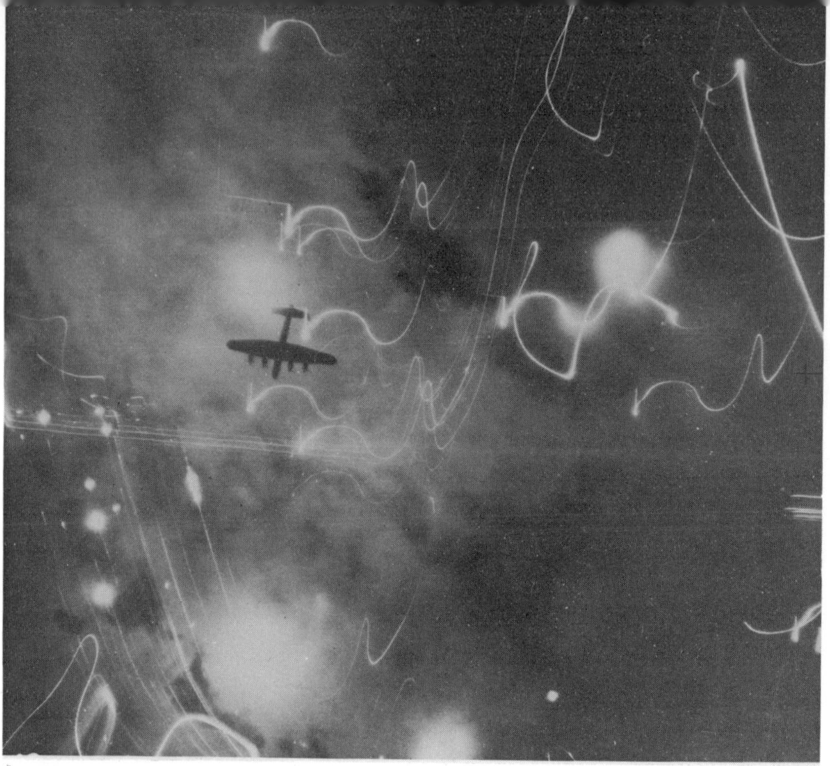

A Lancaster silhouetted against a background of fire and flak during a fire raid on Hamburg. (Imperial War Museum photo)

German transport moving through a 'scorched earth' district in Russia (Imperial War Museum photo)

Fire in War

Incendiary target markers bursting on the roofs of the Gnome and Rhone Aeroengine Works at Limoges. (Imperial War Museum photo)

However his army remained badly outnumbered by the French so they were slowly driven back into Portugal. While they were being driven back Wellington used the time to fortify the lines of the Torres Vedras which stretch across the Peninsula between the River Tagus and the sea. As they fell back, Wellington's army burned everything they had to leave behind, in case it might be useful to the French troops. Once they had got back to their prepared line, Wellington's army settled down to wait in comfort. Their lines of communication were short, the British navy kept up a steady flow of food and supplies to them from home, and they even found time for a bit of hunting. Massena, the French commander, saw that he could not successfully assail these rugged positions so his army settled down to wait, too. By contrast, the French lines of communication were stretched long.

They could not get supplies by sea because the British navy was there. They could find nothing left for them on land because Wellington's army had burned everything useful. Wellington's scorched-earth tactics had succeeded. Baffled, the French army had to leave Portugal altogether in 1811.

Russia has been forced to use these tactics twice within the last two centuries; once against Napoleon and, again, against Hitler.

When Napoleon began his war with Russia in 1812, the Russian forces were only about a half or a third of the strength of Napoleon's and inferior in training. The Russians had no choice but to retreat. As they fell back, they burned and destroyed anything they could not take away, which might be useful to the French, as Wellington had done in Portugal.

After the battle of Borodine, the French forced their way into Moscow — to find it in flames. There Napoleon waited for five weeks, until 19th October, for peace proposals from the Russians. None came. The French lines were again overstretched, they could not support themselves on what was left on the land, their supplies were continually attacked by Cossacks, and winter was coming.

Napoleon withdrew with his army as the snow began to fall, and they suffered terribly during the long struggle home through the cold Russian winter.

Russia was again invaded, in June, 1941, this time at Hitler's orders, by the armies of Nazi Germany. Again the Russians used the enormous size of their country and the 'scorched-earth' policy to defeat their attackers. On 3rd July, Stalin, the Russian leader, ordered his Red Army to destroy everything which could be useful to the enemy, if they were forced back. Even if it meant that Russians left behind had to starve, nothing should be left for the enemy.

During June, July and August, the Germans advanced rapidly into Russia. In September they reached Leningrad, Lakes Ladoga and Onega and moved well into Karelia. The Red Army did what Stalin had commanded, burning houses, food supplies and crops, breaking up railways and blowing up bridges and dams.

In its earlier campaigns, the German armies had lived on the supplies and used the petrol of the countries they had overrun. Now they found themselves unable to live off the country, and with their long supply

Fire in War 175

routes and communications attacked by guerrillas. And the winter was coming.

Towards the end of November the Germans were less than forty miles from Moscow. Exhausted by the strain of fighting and by the cold, they stopped, only to be attacked by the Russian Winter Army. These were specially equipped and trained soldiers, dressed in white, with white tanks and guns. They first held the Germans and then began to force tham back in some places and encircle them in others. Hitler had tried to do what Napoleon had tried before and his army was about to suffer a similar fate.

FIDO

Fog-covered airfields are unusable. During World War II, fire was used to clear English airfields of fog so that R.A.F. planes could take off and land safely. This helped us to keep up the pressure in the air war. The method used was nick-named 'FIDO' (Fog Investigation Dispersal Operation). Burning petrol was squirted out of perforated pipes in rows along the sides of the runways and around the edge of the airfield. The heat from the burning petrol turned the water drops of the fog into invisible water vapour and also swept the fog upwards in the column of rising hot air. The largest areas cleared this way were 2,000 metres long and 250 metres wide. If there was no wind, fog could be completely cleared from an area like this within 5 to 10 minutes after lighting the burners, up to 300 metres or more above the ground. Nowadays, heat from the exhausts of jet engines does the job more economically.

PLACES TO VISIT

If you are in the London area, visit the Imperial War Museum, Lambeth Road, London, S.E.1. Among their interesting collection of weapons and pictures is a collection of flame throwers and photos of them in action.

The various regimental depots in the country have their military museums. Try your nearest one. Whether you find anything directly connected with fire, or not, you should have an interesting visit.

READING

Look through 'Jackdaw' No. 5, *The Armada,* compiled and edited by John Langdon-Davies (Jonathan Cape, 30, Bedford Square, London, W.C.1.).

To find out about the snags of marking targets with incendiaries, and how they were overcome, read *The Dam Busters,* by Paul Brickhill (Pan Books Ltd.)

In *Discoveries, Dinosaurs to Rockets,* Ray Bethers (Constable Young Books, London, 1963) read 'By the rocket's red glare' and 'V-2 for vengeance'.
The Spanish Armada, J. Williams and L. B. Smith (Cassell, London, 1966).
Battle of the Spanish Armada, Roger Hart, The Documentary History Series (Wayland, 1973).